For almost four decades, David Bird's tales of the bridge-crazy monks of St Titus have appeared in magazines around the world.

In this thirteenth collection in book form, the pompous and self-important Abbot returns from his heroics in the Chennai Bermuda Bowl to discover that his fellow monks have taken little interest in this adventure. It is no easy matter for him to endure once again the aggravating ups and downs of life as a bridge player, familiar to us all. The Abbot plays matches and duplicate sessions against a range of colourful opponents. How can it be that a battle-hardened veteran of the Bermuda Bowl cannot always sweep such moderate opposition aside?

Claude Yorke-Smith, his overbearing brother from Devon, pays the monastery a visit. The Abbot spends a week in the Convent of Hilda's and is shocked by the severe attitude of the Mother of Discipline. The Abbot is visited by his partner from Chennai, the Parrot. How will the bridge players of Hampshire react to such a feathered and outspoken opponent?

Regular followers of David Bird's work will know what to expect – a first-rate mixture of amazing bridge, entertaining characters and sparkling dialogue.

THE ABBOT'S RETURN TO EARTH

David Bird

IN ASSOCIATION WITH
PETER CRAWLEY

First published in Great Britain 2016
in association with Peter Crawley
by Weidenfeld & Nicolson
an imprint of the
Orion Publishing Group Ltd
Carmelite House, 50 Victoria Embankment
London EC4Y 0DZ

An Hachette UK Company

10 9 8 7 6 5 4 3 2 1

A CIP catalogue record for this book is
available from the British Library.

ISBN (Trade Paperback) 978 1 474 60378 2

Typeset at The Spartan Press Ltd, Lymington, Hampshire

Printed in Great Britain by Clays Ltd, St Ives plc

MIX
Paper from
responsible sources
FSC
www.fsc.org FSC® C104740

www.orionbooks.co.uk

Contents

Once again I would like to thank my great friend and fellow writer, Tim Bourke of Australia. Acknowledged as the world's finest constructor of bridge deals, he gave me many of the most unusual and imaginative deals in this book.

DB

Part I The Return from Chennai

1.   Back to Basics

Brother Hubert, the monastery janitor, unlocked the iron front gate. 'Ah, you're back, Abbot,' he said. 'It's great to see you again!'

The two monks took the long walk to the main building. 'Goodness me, these suitcases are heavy,' exclaimed Brother Hubert. 'Did you bring back some duty-free bottles?'

'I had a large number of copies printed of the Bermuda Bowl bulletins,' replied the Abbot. 'They make inspiring reading, I can tell you. We'll need a full set for the monastery archives too.'

'Did you enjoy the event?' asked Brother Hubert. 'I wouldn't mind watching for a couple of hours. Any longer and I'd find it a bit boring, really.'

'Watching?' exclaimed the Abbot. 'Have you not seen the emails that I sent? I was playing in it!'

'Not in the main Bermuda Bowl event, surely?' queried Brother Hubert. 'I thought that was just for experts.'

The Abbot strode into the main building, disappointed that his reception had been somewhat less than ticker-tape. What was the point of sending email after email all the way from India when nobody bothered to read them?

The Abbot had no intention of missing the Thursday night duplicate, despite his exhaustion from the long return flight on Air India. His first opponents were Brother Aelred and Brother Michael. An amusing thought occurred to him – there could hardly be a greater contrast between the present opposition and the last pair he had faced at the table: the legendary Jeff Meckstroth and Eric Rodwell!

This was the first board of the evening:

Both Vul.   ♠ Q 6
Dealer South   ♡ K Q 8 5 3 2
                ◇ 8 2
                ♣ Q 7 6

♠ 9 3	N	♠ J 10 4
♡ 10 9 6	W E	♡ J 7 4
◇ A K Q 10 9 5	S	◇ 7 6
♣ J 4		♣ K 10 9 5 2

                ♠ A K 8 7 5 2
                ♡ A
                ◇ J 4 3
                ♣ A 8 3

WEST	NORTH	EAST	SOUTH
Brother	*Brother*	*Brother*	*The*
Michael	*Xavier*	*Aelred*	*Abbot*
–	–	–	1♠
2◇	2♡	Pass	3♠
Pass	4♠	All Pass	

Brother Michael began with the ace and king of diamonds, his partner playing high-low. The Abbot paused for thought when the ◇Q was led at Trick 3. If he ruffed low in the dummy, even a moderate performer such as Brother Aelred might return a trump after over-ruffing. That would kill the entry to dummy while the hearts were blocked.

How about allowing the ◇Q to win, discarding a club? The defenders would not then have the opportunity to dislodge the trump queen entry. Still, if East held only three hearts, he could discard one. Give him three trumps as well and he would be able to prevent a second club discard on dummy's hearts.

The Abbot decided to try something different. 'Ruff with the queen,' he said.

Brother Aelred discarded a heart on this trick and the Abbot drew two rounds of trumps with the ace and king. He then cashed the ♡A and threw East on lead with a third round of trumps. Seeing that a heart exit would allow a quick claim of the remaining tricks, Brother Aelred returned the ♣9.

The Abbot ran this successfully to dummy's ♣Q and was then able to claim the contract. 'Memories of the Bermuda Bowl come flooding back,' he said. 'Even the great Geir Helgemo would have admired that line of play.'

'If Helgemo had been East, I think he would have beaten it,' remarked Brother Xavier. 'What happens if Brother Aelred underruffs with the jack or ten on the third round of diamonds?'

The Abbot waved this suggestion aside. It was typical of Xavier to seek some distraction rather than praising his partner's efforts.

'You can't throw him in on the third round of trumps then,' Brother Xavier continued. 'If you try ace and a low trump instead, playing for the remaining trumps to be 2-2, East can unblock his other honour on the first round and West wins the second round with the ♠9.'

The Abbot raised his eyebrows. Did Brother Xavier realize how foolish he sounded? No creature on God's earth was less likely to find a double trump unblock than the present East player.

A round or two later, the unruly novices Brother Cameron and Brother Damien took their seats against the Abbot. On the first deal they scored above average, making a straightforward spade game. This was the next board:

North-South Vul.
Dealer North

```
              ♠ A 6 4
              ♡ A Q 6
              ◇ 10 8
              ♣ K 10 8 5 2
♠ Q J 10 8 2                ♠ K 9 7 3
♡ K 7         N              ♡ J 9 5
◇ K J 5 2    W   E           ◇ Q 9 7
♣ 6 3           S            ♣ Q J 9
              ♠ 5
              ♡ 10 8 4 3 2
              ◇ A 6 4 3
              ♣ A 7 4
```

WEST	NORTH	EAST	SOUTH
Brother	*Brother*	*The*	*Brother*
Xavier	*Damien*	*Abbot*	*Cameron*
–	1♣	Pass	1♡
1♠	Dble	3♠	4♡
All Pass			

Brother Damien indicated three hearts with a Support Double. When the Abbot raised partner's spade overcall to the three-level, Brother Cameron had no hesitation in bidding the heart game. With any luck, the opponents would sacrifice at this score. If not, was there any law against partner putting down a useful hand?

There was no further bidding and Brother Xavier led the ♠Q. 'Yeah, that's good,' said Brother Cameron as the dummy appeared. 'Ace up!'

The Abbot winced at the novice's disrespectful tone. Was this any way to speak at the bridge table? Not when you were facing a Bermuda Bowl veteran.

Brother Cameron reached his hand with the ♣A and finessed the ♡Q successfully. He cashed the ♡A, finding a 3-2 break, and ducked a second round of clubs. The Abbot won with the ♣J and had no successful return. If he drew a third round of trumps with the jack, declarer would reach dummy with the ♣K and discard two diamond losers on the clubs. If instead he returned a club and ruffed the fourth round of clubs with the jack, dummy's last trump would be brought back to life.

With little hope of success, the Abbot switched to the ◇7. Brother Cameron won with the ace, crossed to the ♣K and called for another club. He then faced his cards, claiming ten tricks.

The Abbot shook his head as he returned his cards to the wallet. It was hard to imagine a more impertinent bid from the novice. Four Hearts, he says, holding only five low trumps and two aces. Needless to say, all the cards lay perfectly and the game was lay-down. Typical!

Brother Damien looked surprised as he inspected the score sheet. 'No-one else bid it,' he reported.

'Four Hearts was a two-way bid,' explained Brother Cameron. 'I was hoping for a sacrifice.'

On the next round two more novices arrived at the Abbot's table. Polite and respectful in every way, Brother Daniel and Brother Simon set a fine example to the rest of the novitiate. The hapless Brother Cameron could learn a lot from them.

'Did you enjoy playing in the Bermuda Bowl, Abbot?' asked the dark-haired Brother Daniel.

Pleased by the question, the Abbot nodded his head. 'It's quite an experience, playing in an event where every opponent is world-class,' he replied. 'I can scarcely remember anyone making a mistake against us.'

Brother Simon looked at the Abbot somewhat nervously. 'We'll try our best,' he said.

'You mustn't worry at all,' the Abbot informed him. 'Bridge is always a difficult game at first. It took me many years to reach international standard.'

The players extracted their cards for this deal:

Both Vul.
Dealer East

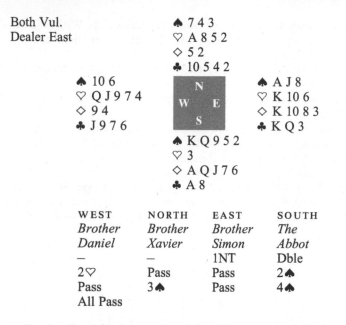

```
                  ♠ 7 4 3
                  ♡ A 8 5 2
                  ◇ 5 2
                  ♣ 10 5 4 2
   ♠ 10 6                          ♠ A J 8
   ♡ Q J 9 7 4                     ♡ K 10 6
   ◇ 9 4                           ◇ K 10 8 3
   ♣ J 9 7 6                       ♣ K Q 3
                  ♠ K Q 9 5 2
                  ♡ 3
                  ◇ A Q J 7 6
                  ♣ A 8
```

WEST	NORTH	EAST	SOUTH
Brother	*Brother*	*Brother*	*The*
Daniel	*Xavier*	*Simon*	*Abbot*
–	–	1NT	Dble
2♡	Pass	Pass	2♠
Pass	3♠	Pass	4♠
All Pass			

Brother Daniel led the ♡Q and the Abbot surveyed the dummy with no obvious enthusiasm. Three trumps, only one good card and ten losers in the hand? Was that enough for a raise? Not as he saw it. Mind you, different standards had to be followed when your partner was a Bermuda Bowl player.

'Play the ace,' said the Abbot. A finesse of the ◇Q succeeded and he continued with the ◇A, the ◇9 appearing on his left. When the ◇6 was led to the next trick, Brother Daniel paused to consider his defence. His ten of trumps was higher than the seven in dummy. Would the Abbot be cross if he ruffed with it? Well, he would soon find out!

Brother Daniel ruffed with the ♠10 and the Abbot threw a heart from dummy. He ruffed the heart continuation and led the ◇7. West discarded a heart and the Abbot ruffed in the dummy. A trump to the nine won the next trick and the Abbot continued with the trump king. A few moments later the game was his.

Ah well, thought Brother Daniel, at least the Abbot hadn't got cross when he ruffed the third diamond.

The Abbot turned to his left. 'You shouldn't have ruffed with the ten,' he exclaimed.

Brother Daniel looked downwards. 'Sorry, Abbot,' he replied.

'Discard instead and I ruff in the dummy,' continued the Abbot. 'Suppose I reach my hand with a heart ruff and lead another diamond.

Now you ruff with the ten and exit with a heart or a club. With no entry left to the dummy, I have to lose two further trump tricks to your partner. Do you see?'

It was way beyond Brother Daniel's mental powers to follow this analysis. 'Ah yes,' he replied.

The final visitors to the Abbot's table were Brother Lucius and Brother Paulo.

'What a marvellous time you must have had in Chennai!' Brother Lucius exclaimed. 'We could hardly believe some of the hands you played against USA-1 in the final match.'

'One does one's best,' the Abbot replied.

'It was almost like a fairy tale for you and the Upper Bhumpopo team to beat the USA,' Brother Lucius continued. 'If it was written up in a bridge magazine or some bridge book, you wouldn't believe it!'

The players drew their cards for this board:

Neither Vul.
Dealer South

	♠ A Q 9	
	♡ A 10 6 2	
	◇ J 9 2	
	♣ A K 8	
♠ K J 10 8 7	N	♠ 6 5 4 2
♡ K Q J 9 4 3	W E	♡ 8 7 5
◇ –	S	◇ Q 10 8
♣ Q 4		♣ J 10 7
	♠ 3	
	♡ –	
	◇ A K 7 6 5 4 3	
	♣ 9 6 5 3 2	

WEST	NORTH	EAST	SOUTH
Brother	*Brother*	*The*	*Brother*
Xavier	*Paulo*	*Abbot*	*Lucius*
–	–	–	3◇
4◇	6◇	All Pass	
All Pass			

Brother Lucius ruffed the ♡K lead in his hand and played the ace of trumps, West discarding a heart. So, he had a trump loser. How could he avoid losing a club trick too? A successful spade finesse would give him eleven tricks. Suppose he gave up a trump trick. Would there then be a chance of squeezing West in the majors? If the Abbot was still in his Chennai form, he could break up any such squeeze when he took his trump trick. He could return a spade into dummy's ace-queen and there would then be no link to the dummy.

Brother Lucius decided to try something different. He finessed the ♠Q successfully and cashed the ♠A, throwing a club. He then ruffed the last spade in his hand. Returning to dummy with the ♣K, he discarded another club on the ♡A and ruffed a heart in his hand. A club to dummy's ace left these cards still to be played:

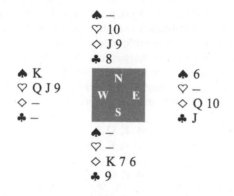

'Play the ♡10, please,' said Brother Lucius.

If the Abbot ruffed this trick, Lucius would simply discard his club loser and score three trump tricks. Nor was a discard of the master club any good. Declarer would ruff and play the established club, leaving East to score just a trump trick. With a small shrug, the Abbot discarded a spade. Brother Lucius ruffed in his hand and exited with a club. The Abbot won with the jack and had to lead into declarer's split trump tenace. The slam had been made.

'Xavier held all the major-suit cards,' observed Brother Lucius, turning towards the Abbot. 'A simpler line was to exit with a trump early on. My fear was that you would break up the squeeze with a spade return into the ace-queen.'

With a sigh the Abbot returned his cards to the board. 'Indeed I would have done,' he replied. 'No other defence would make any sense at all!'

2. The Abbot's Expedition

'Ah, good morning, Abbot,' said Brother Lucius, shielding his eyes from the sunlight pervading the cloisters. 'Did Xavier tell me that you're playing bridge in the village tonight?'

'I can hardly spare the time,' the Abbot replied. 'It's a national simultaneous for Children in Need, a very good cause.'

Brother Lucius maintained a straight face. 'Yes, and there should be a bundle of masterpoints available too.'

The Abbot smiled at this suggestion. 'I hardly think that's of any relevance,' he declared. 'Not for a Bermuda Bowl man.'

The clock in Hursley Church was striking seven as the game began in the village hall. This was an early board at the Abbot's table.

North-South Vul.
Dealer North

```
                 ♠ K Q 5
                 ♡ A K 7 3
                 ◇ A K J 5
                 ♣ K Q
   ♠ 10 9 8 4 3 2           ♠ J 6
   ♡ 8 5 4 2         N      ♡ —
   ◇ 7            W     E   ◇ Q 10 9 8 6 3
   ♣ 9 2             S      ♣ A J 10 8 4
                 ♠ A 7
                 ♡ Q J 10 9 6
                 ◇ 4 2
                 ♣ 7 6 5 3
```

WEST	NORTH	EAST	SOUTH
Daphne	*Brother*	*Grace*	*The*
Lucas	*Xavier*	*Chandler*	*Abbot*
—	2♣	2NT	3♡
Pass	4NT	Pass	5◇
Pass	6♡	All Pass	

The elderly East player overcalled 2NT, alerted by her partner, and the Abbot bid 3♡ without any pause.

The somewhat frail-looking Daphne Lucas leaned forward. 'You didn't give me time to explain the 2NT,' she said. 'It's not natural, it shows both the . . .'

'I didn't ask for an explanation,' intervened the Abbot. 'You don't have to explain a bid unless the opponents ask about it.'

Daphne Lucas surveyed the Abbot disapprovingly. What a rude person! Not only was he a man of the cloth, he was also a guest at the club. Good manners were surely not too much to expect.

West led her singleton diamond against the eventual 6♡ and the Abbot surveyed the dummy happily. Unless trumps were 4-0 the slam would be a trivial make. He could discard one club loser and ruff the other in the dummy. 'Ace, please,' he said.

When the Abbot drew a round of trumps with the ace, unwelcome news arrived. Trumps were indeed 4-0. What could be done? If he gave up a club, preparing for a club ruff, there was an appreciable risk of a diamond ruff. How about drawing all the trumps and playing to squeeze East? Yes, that should work.

The Abbot drew trumps in four rounds. Playing a club next would lead to defeat – East would return a club and no squeeze would be possible. Instead the Abbot played the ace and king of spades. The ♦K confirmed that West had started with a singleton in the suit and these cards remained:

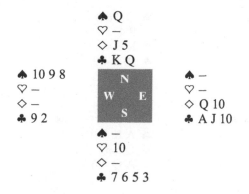

East had no good discard on the ♠Q. If she threw a diamond, declarer would ruff a diamond to establish the ♦J. He would then be able to set up a club entry to the dummy. Grace Chandler eventually decided to throw a club. 'King of clubs, please,' said the Abbot.

When East won with the club ace, she could not safely play a diamond. She returned a club to dummy's queen, unblocking the suit for declarer, and the Abbot claimed the remainder. 'I ruff a diamond to my hand,' he said, 'and this last club is good.'

'Nicely played, Abbot,' said Brother Xavier.

The Abbot nodded. Yes, even by his standards it had been a special effort. He turned towards the lady in the East seat. 'Any expert player would make the slam after your overcall,' he informed her. 'It gave me a complete blueprint of the hand.'

Grace Chandler peered at the Abbot. 'The Unusual No-trump is part of our system,' she replied. 'You don't play it?'

'Everyone plays the Unusual No-trump,' said the Abbot. 'I was just pointing out that on this occasion it assisted me in the play.'

This was too much for Daphne Lucas. 'I hope you don't mind me mentioning this,' she said, 'but we rather pride ourselves on the friendly game here. It may be different at your club but we avoid criticizing anyone's bidding or play.'

'Daphne's the club secretary,' observed Grace Chandler, hoping to add weight to her partner's observation.

The Abbot sat back in his chair. He hadn't said anything critical, had he? If a novice back at St Titus made such a foolish overcall, he would have been much less restrained. How could these ladies learn to play better if no-one pointed out their mistakes?

A round or two later, the Abbot faced two earnest-looking men. This was the first board of the round:

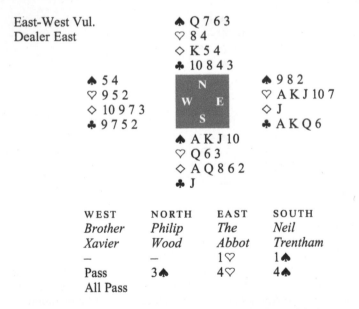

East-West Vul.
Dealer East

North: ♠ Q 7 6 3 ♡ 8 4 ◇ K 5 4 ♣ 10 8 4 3

West: ♠ 5 4 ♡ 9 5 2 ◇ 10 9 7 3 ♣ 9 7 5 2

East: ♠ 9 8 2 ♡ A K J 10 7 ◇ J ♣ A K Q 6

South: ♠ A K J 10 ♡ Q 6 3 ◇ A Q 8 6 2 ♣ J

WEST	NORTH	EAST	SOUTH
Brother	*Philip*	*The*	*Neil*
Xavier	*Wood*	*Abbot*	*Trentham*
—	—	1♡	1♠
Pass	3♠	4♡	4♠
All Pass			

Brother Xavier led the ♡5 and down went the dummy. Good gracious, thought the Abbot. Only five points for a jump raise? He might as well be playing against Brother Cameron. 'Very nice, Philip,' said the 30-year-old declarer. 'Play low, will you?'

The Abbot won with the ♡K and switched to the ♣K. The ♣J fell from declarer and Xavier played the ♣7, which showed an even number of cards in the suit. Concluding that declarer held only one club, the Abbot cashed the ♡A before playing the ♣A. Neil Trentham ruffed in his hand and drew two rounds of trumps. When everyone followed, the Abbot cast a disapproving glance towards the declarer. Only four spades for the overcall? Brother Cameron might be partnering himself at this table.

With the diamonds breaking 4-1, it would have been a fatal move to draw the last trump. Instead Neil Trentham crossed to dummy with the ◇K, the jack falling on his right. He then led the ♣10, covered by the queen and ruffed with his last trump. These cards remained:

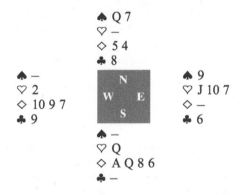

```
                    ♠ Q 7
                    ♡ —
                    ◇ 5 4
                    ♣ 8
  ♠ —                              ♠ 9
  ♡ 2          N                   ♡ J 10 7
  ◇ 10 9 7   W   E                 ◇ —
  ♣ 9            S                 ♣ 6
                    ♠ —
                    ♡ Q
                    ◇ A Q 8 6
                    ♣ —
```

Declarer now led the ♡Q from his hand. Rather than throw dummy's losing club on this trick, he ruffed with the ♠7 and drew the Abbot's last trump. Brother Xavier was pressed for a discard on this trick. Since he had to retain his ♣9, to guard the club threat in dummy, he released one of his diamonds.

Neil Trentham faced his last four cards, all diamonds. 'These must be good now,' he said.

The Abbot blinked. No way had the inexperienced declarer known what he was doing, leading that ♣10, but he had actually transferred the club guard to West and set up a squeeze! Talk about a monkey typing the Bible by accident. It was unbelievable.

'Just the ten, was it?' enquired Philip Wood.

'Yes,' his partner replied. 'I had three top losers. I needed the transfer squeeze just to make game.'

The Abbot glared at his young opponent. Transfer squeeze, did he say? What on earth was such a strong player doing, playing a charity pairs in some obscure village hall? He was obviously an obsessive master-point gatherer – probably driven all the way from London to find a weak heat. Did he not realize the charitable purpose of the event?

Near the end of the first half, the Abbot and Xavier faced a married couple in their mid-sixties. Since his retirement from the local electricity board, Gordon Pearce had been an avid reader of bridge books. With little encouragement from his wife, he had done his best to pass on to her the knowledge he had accumulated.

This was the first board of the round:

```
North-South Vul.              ♠ J 6 5
Dealer West                   ♡ 7 6
                              ◇ A K 9 5 4 2
                              ♣ A K
       ♠ K Q              N            ♠ A 10 9 8 2
       ♡ K Q J                         ♡ 9 5 2
       ◇ J 10 8 3     W       E        ◇ –
       ♣ Q J 8 5          S            ♣ 10 9 6 3 2
                              ♠ 7 4 3
                              ♡ A 10 8 4 3
                              ◇ Q 7 6
                              ♣ 7 4
```

WEST	NORTH	EAST	SOUTH
The	*Judy*	*Brother*	*Gordon*
Abbot	*Pearce*	*Xavier*	*Pearce*
1NT	Dble	2♠	2NT
Pass	3NT	All Pass	

The Abbot reached for the ♠K but Gordon Pearce stopped him. 'My wife should have alerted 2NT,' he said. 'It was Lebensohl.'

Judy Pearce looked up in some alarm. 'I didn't bid a no-trump, Gordon,' she said. 'This man here did.'

'Yes, but Lebensohl applies opposite a double of 1NT too,' her husband informed her. 'Logically, it's the same situation.'

'I'm leading this card anyway,' declared the Abbot.

'I took 2NT as natural,' said Judy Pearce, laying out the dummy. 'Still, it's only pairs. If the spades are bare, it's only a bottom.'

The ♠K won the first trick and the Abbot continued with the ♠Q, which also won. It was typical of this hopeless pair's luck that the spade suit was blocked. The best chance now was surely to dislodge the ♡A before declarer discovered the diamond situation.

Gordon Pearce won the ♡K switch with the ♡A and led the ◇6, the Abbot following in bored fashion with the ◇3. 'Play the nine, please,' said the declarer.

Judy Pearce looked puzzled but a big smile came to her face when East showed out. 'Well played, Gordon,' she said.

'Nine tricks are there now,' said Gordon Pearce.

The Abbot's mouth fell open. How on earth had declarer taken such an inspired view of the diamond suit?

Gordon Pearce looked towards the Abbot. 'That's right, isn't it? Six diamonds, the ♡A and the ♣A-K.'

'I'm perfectly capable of counting up to nine,' the Abbot retorted. 'How did you manage to read the diamond situation?'

'I could hardly ignore the odds,' Pearce replied. 'You had two spades, so your 1NT marked you with 4-4-3-2 shape. There was a 2-to-1 chance that diamonds would be one of your four-card suits.'

The Abbot blinked. 'That's not right,' he said. 'I was bound to hold four clubs or my partner would have six and would have bid 2♣ instead of 2♠.'

'Not necessarily,' Pearce replied.

'Apart from that, there were six hearts out and only four diamonds,' continued the Abbot. 'The odds were huge that I would hold four hearts rather than four diamonds.'

'The diamond finesse might win even if you held only three diamonds,' said Gordon Pearce. 'Since I started reading so many bridge books, I've taken a lot more finesses, I can tell you.'

'It's a top for us,' said Mrs Pearce, gazing admiringly at the scoresheet. 'I don't think we'd have got there without Lebensohl!'

3. The Abbot's Helpful Remarks

The Abbot tapped a finger down his column of estimated scores as the half-time pots of tea were served. Only half a top above average? It defied belief in a club of this standard. He consulted his watch more than once as the tea-break stretched out to a full 15 minutes. Was this a bridge club or some sort of social club? The two ladies at his table had done nothing but compare notes on the various ailments of the club members.

'Time for the second half, everyone!' called the posh-voiced Ethel Clowder eventually. 'Don't forget to wash your tea cups when you take them back to the kitchen. Last week there were two unwashed cups.'

Good gracious, thought the Abbot. This was probably the most exciting thing that had happened here all year. Surprising it hadn't made the local paper, really.

The second half began with the Abbot facing an elderly couple.

North-South Vul.
Dealer South

	♠ 7 6 4	
	♡ K 8 5	
	◇ A 10 8 2	
	♣ 8 7 2	
♠ 10 3		♠ 8 5 2
♡ Q 10 7 3		♡ A J 9
◇ J 9 5		◇ Q 7 6
♣ J 10 6 4		♣ Q 9 5 3
	♠ A K Q J 9	
	♡ 6 4 2	
	◇ K 4 3	
	♣ A K	

WEST	NORTH	EAST	SOUTH
Stan	*Brother*	*Betty*	*The*
Lucraft	*Xavier*	*Lucraft*	*Abbot*
–	–	–	1♠
Pass	2♠	Pass	4♠
All Pass			

'My lead, is it?' asked Stan Lucraft, whose wayward grey hair was badly in need of a cut.

On receiving a nod from his wife, he led the ♡3. Betty Lucraft won with the ♡J and switched to a trump. The Abbot drew trumps in three rounds and paused to consider his prospects. If diamonds were 3-3, the suit would provide a discard. He would have to duck a diamond into the safe East hand, of course, otherwise a further heart lead from West would damage him.

At Trick 5 the Abbot led the ◇2. Stan Lucraft leaned forward to inspect the dummy's diamond holding. He then went in with the ◇J. The Abbot winced. Did West hold the ◇Q as well? Surely the old codger hadn't found the brilliancy of inserting the jack from ◇J-x-x? It was annoying, anyway. He would have to play dummy's ace and the entry to the thirteenth diamond would be gone.

The Abbot won with the ◇A and returned to his hand with the ◇K, hoping to see the other diamond honour appear from West. When no such luck materialized, he played his remaining trumps. This was the position with one trump still to be played:

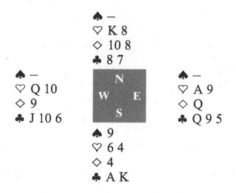

The Abbot led ♠9, throwing a club from dummy. Betty Lucraft fingered her remaining cards thoughtfully in the East seat. Surely all the red-suit cards were needed. In that case she would have to throw a club. The Abbot continued with the ♣A-K and exited with his last diamond, fully expecting West to win with the queen and put a lethal second heart through dummy's king. To his amazement it was East who won the trick. Betty Lucraft had to play ace and another heart and dummy's ♡K gave the Abbot his tenth trick.

'Dummy play of the highest order!' exclaimed the Abbot. He turned towards the West player. 'That was good defence putting in the ◇J. Against any other declarer in the room, you would have beaten the contract.'

'Yes, I read about that play only last night,' replied Stan Lucraft. 'It's called an uppercut. The jack forced out dummy's ace and promoted Betty's queen.'

'Ah, an uppercut,' said Betty Lucraft, looking admiringly at her husband. 'We live and learn.'

Brother Xavier unrolled the score sheet. 'It's a mixture of 420s and 430s,' he reported. 'Well below average for us, I'm afraid.'

'What?' said the Abbot, leaning forward. 'I had to stand on my head to make ten tricks after that ◇J play.'

Stan Lucraft smiled happily. 'Not many of our members will understand the uppercut,' he observed. 'The other Wests probably played low and partner's queen was never promoted.'

On the next round the Abbot faced two elderly ladies. Had a prize been available for the oldest competitors in the event, they would have been definite front runners. This was the first board:

Both Vul.
Dealer South

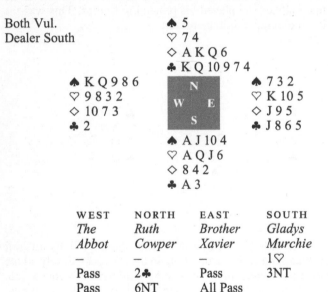

```
                    ♠ 5
                    ♡ 7 4
                    ◇ A K Q 6
                    ♣ K Q 10 9 7 4
  ♠ K Q 9 8 6                      ♠ 7 3 2
  ♡ 9 8 3 2            N           ♡ K 10 5
  ◇ 10 7 3         W     E         ◇ J 9 5
  ♣ 2                 S            ♣ J 8 6 5
                    ♠ A J 10 4
                    ♡ A Q J 6
                    ◇ 8 4 2
                    ♣ A 3
```

WEST	NORTH	EAST	SOUTH
The	*Ruth*	*Brother*	*Gladys*
Abbot	*Cowper*	*Xavier*	*Murchie*
—	—	—	1♡
Pass	2♣	Pass	3NT
Pass	6NT	All Pass	

The Abbot led the ♠K and Ruth Cowper laid out her dummy somewhat untidily. 'I hope this is enough,' she said 'I added three length-points for the clubs.'

'Very nice, partner,' Gladys Murchie replied. 'It's a good method, adding points for length. 6NT would have been hopeless if you held only two or three clubs.'

The Abbot restrained himself from comment. As a rough guide, he reckoned his blood pressure rose by about 1% for every word the opponents exchanged before the first card was played from dummy. Newspaper pundits might think that mountaineering or powerboat racing were more of a health risk. They'd soon change their minds if they ever played bridge.

'I took it that you had a spade cover when you called no-trump,' continued Ruth Cowper.

The elderly declarer won with the ♠A and paused to count her top tricks. Six clubs, three diamonds and two major-suit aces. That was — how many was it? — eleven tricks. The safest way of setting up a twelfth trick was surely to return the ♠J. Yes, if the fat man won with the queen, her ten would be good. If he held up, the jack would be a winner! 6NT bid and made should be a nice top.

The Abbot won the ♠J with the queen and declarer discarded a heart from dummy. When he returned the ♠9, she threw a diamond from dummy and won in her hand with the ♠10. She then played the ace and king of clubs, preparing to claim the contract.

'Oh no!' exclaimed Gladys Murchie, as the Abbot showed out on the second round of clubs. 'That's very bad luck, Ruth. I had it made on a normal club break.'

Declarer had to concede a club trick and ended one down. Few other pairs had ventured so high and it was a poor score for the ladies. 'It's a pity you weren't sitting North-South,' Ruth Cowper informed the Abbot. 'You would probably have bid the slam and we'd have scored a nice top.'

The Abbot chuckled to himself. 'I don't think minus 1440 would have been a top for you,' he replied.

The two ladies glared at the Abbot. Was he suggesting that the slam should have been made? What a rude man!

The Abbot turned towards the white-haired declarer. 'You should have tested the clubs first, by playing the king and ace,' he informed her. 'Once you know that the clubs are breaking badly, you can lead the ♠J and throw a club from dummy. You throw another club on the spade return and can then take advantage of the favourable lie in the red suits.'

Ruth Cowper had rarely encountered such an obnoxious person. Such a loud voice, too. Did he want the whole room to hear how clever he was? 'Was the ♡K onside, then?' she enquired.

'Yes, that gives you three heart tricks,' boomed the Abbot, 'and diamonds break 3-3 too.'

'Ssshh!' said someone from an adjacent table.

Ruth Cowper rarely spoke back when anyone was rude to her. This man was too much, though. Someone needed to tell him how to behave or he would go on being rude for the rest of his life. She summoned up her courage. 'Is it normal to criticize other players in the club where you play?' she said. 'It isn't here in the village. A friendly atmosphere makes the game so much more enjoyable.'

'That's right,' her partner added. 'In any case, the way Ruth played it only needed a 3-2 club break. Your line would need a 3-3 diamond break and a finesse. I'm not saying it's a bad line, mind you. I wouldn't be so rude as to say anything like that.'

'Move for the next round,' called a shrill voice.

Looking somewhat stunned, the Abbot left the table. He had rarely played in such an inhospitable club. This was the second time that he'd been criticized for making helpful remarks. The players seemed to make no attempt to welcome guests to their club.

The final round saw the Abbot facing a retired couple, Herbert and Evelyn Parker.

Neither Vul.
Dealer South

```
                    ♠ K Q 6 5
                    ♡ A 9 7 5
                    ◇ 8 3
                    ♣ K 8 5
   ♠ 10 2                          ♠ 8 7 3
   ♡ 10 8           N              ♡ K Q J 2
   ◇ J 7 5 4 2    W   E            ◇ 9
   ♣ J 10 9 6       S              ♣ Q 7 4 3 2
                    ♠ A J 9 4
                    ♡ 6 4 3
                    ◇ A K Q 10 6
                    ♣ A
```

WEST	NORTH	EAST	SOUTH
Herbert	*Brother*	*Evelyn*	*The*
Parker	*Xavier*	*Parker*	*Abbot*
—	—	—	1◇
Pass	1♡	Pass	1♠
Pass	4♠	Pass	6♠
All Pass			

A straightforward auction carried the monastery pair to a small slam and the ♣J was led. The Abbot won with the bare ace and drew trumps, pleased to see the suit break 3-2. If the ◇J fell in three rounds he would score an overtrick. If diamonds divided 4-2 and the jack didn't fall, he would have to settle for twelve tricks. He could establish the thirteenth diamond and throw one of his hearts on the ♣K.

The Abbot cashed the ace and king of diamonds and could not believe his eyes when East showed out on the second round. What appalling bad luck! The only remaining chance was to find a 3-3 heart break. After throwing one heart on the club king he would then be able to ruff the thirteenth heart good.

The Abbot ducked a heart, preparing to follow this line. No 3-3 break materialized in the suit and he was one down. 'Unbelievable bad luck,' he declared. 'A 5-1 diamond break and a 4-2 heart break.'

'Yes, you were a bit unlucky,' said Evelyn Parker.

Brother Xavier inspected the score sheet. 'No-one else bid the slam,' he said. 'It's a mixture of 450s and 480s.'

'Some declarers made twelve tricks?' exclaimed the Abbot. 'It's not possible, surely.'

'Very difficult, it's true,' said Evelyn Parker. 'You can set up four diamond tricks, can't you? When my nine falls, you have to lead low to the eight on the second round.'

The Abbot's mouth fell open. The ◇8 had been in dummy, had it? And the ◇9 had fallen on the first round? He hadn't even seen the card. No doubt this woman had turned it over quickly. It would be typical of the sharp practice at this club.

'I thought you must be missing the ◇10,' said Brother Xavier. 'It's obvious to set up an extra trick in diamonds, isn't it?'

'And lose the pairs overtrick when East holds ◇J-9 or has false-carded from ◇J-9-x?' demanded the Abbot. 'I might have employed the safety play, I suppose, in a club where everyone is reluctant to bid slams. In a World Pairs championship every single declarer would follow my line.' He smiled to himself as he returned his cards to the wallet. 'It would be absurd not to!'

4.   The Inspector Calls

Every now and again, the Abbot participated in the Tuesday duplicate session in the novitiate. Parading his superior skill at the game was a good way of gaining respect among the novices. Meanwhile, he was able to check that the youngsters were not indulging in any conventions unsuited to their abilities. For example, what could be more absurd than allowing anyone under 21 to play Exclusion Blackwood? On the present occasion the Abbot was partnering the reasonably competent Brother Damien and had just managed to score an overtrick in 3NT.

'Well played, Abbot,' said Brother Damien, who knew what was expected of him.

The Abbot nodded. 'I played a similar hand in the Bermuda Bowl, I recall.'

This was the next deal:

```
Neither Vul.              ♠ A J 10 2
Dealer East               ♡ —
                          ◇ Q J 10 9 6 3 2
                          ♣ 7 5
     ♠ K 8 7 5 4 3              N              ♠ 9
     ♡ Q 8                                     ♡ A K J 9 7 5 4
     ◇ 7 5             W              E        ◇ A K 8 4
     ♣ K 10 3                                  ♣ Q
                               S
                          ♠ Q 6
                          ♡ 10 6 3 2
                          ◇ —
                          ♣ A J 9 8 6 4 2
```

WEST	NORTH	EAST	SOUTH
The	*Brother*	*Brother*	*Brother*
Abbot	*Duncan*	*Damien*	*Adam*
—	—	1♡	3♣
Pass	4♣	4♡	5♣
Dble	All Pass		

The Abbot led the ♡Q, not overjoyed to see dummy go down with a void heart. Brother Adam ruffed in the dummy and called for the ◇Q. East covered with the king and he ruffed in his hand.

The Abbot winced at the cards played to this trick. It seemed that the defenders' 17 points in the red suits were to be ruffed into oblivion.

Where was the justice in that? Also, why did Brother Damien think it appropriate to play the ◇K from his A-K combination? It might make no difference on this particular deal but surely the ace was a better card, leaving declarer in doubt as to who held the king.

Brother Adam ruffed another heart in dummy and called for the ◇J. After a few moments Brother Damien decided to play low, not fancying the defenders' chances if the diamonds were established. It seemed natural for declarer to discard a heart on this trick, but Brother Adam saw that there might be potential problems subsequently. Since he needed the spade finesse to be right anyway, he decided to ruff this trick.

Back in his hand, the young declarer played the ace of trumps on which East's queen appeared. He then led the ♠Q. The Abbot declined to cover and the card was run successfully. A spade to the jack left these cards still to be played:

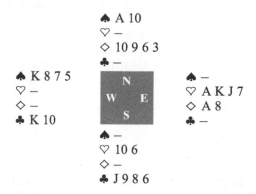

          ♠ A 10
          ♡ —
          ◇ 10 9 6 3
          ♣ —
♠ K 8 7 5   ♠ —
♡ —   ♡ A K J 7
◇ —   ◇ A 8
♣ K 10   ♣ —
          ♠ —
          ♡ 10 6
          ◇ —
          ♣ J 9 8 6

Brother Adam, who had not yet lost a trick, ruffed another diamond in his hand. Seeing his fate if he overruffed, the Abbot discarded a spade. He was thrown on lead with a trump to the ten and had to concede defeat. Whether or not he cashed the king of trumps first, he would have to play a spade. Declarer would finesse dummy's ten and cash the ace, ditching his two remaining heart losers. Eleven tricks could not be prevented.

'Very unlucky for us,' muttered the Abbot. 'I didn't think much of your ◇K play, partner.'

Brother Adam nodded and turned towards Brother Damien. 'The Abbot's right,' he said. 'If you play low on the first round of diamonds, allowing dummy's queen to win, that beats the contract. I can throw one heart on the trick but you cover the second round of diamonds and I have to ruff. When I ruff a second heart and lead the ◇10, covered again, the Abbot overruffs me and switches to the ♠K while you still have a trump.'

'That's exactly what I would have done,' declared the Abbot, who was struggling to follow this analysis. Ah yes, declarer would then be locked in dummy and would either suffer a spade ruff or the loss of two further trump tricks. Some of these youngsters knew more about the game than you might expect.

Brother Damien shrugged his shoulders. Play low on the first round of diamonds? Who on earth would do that? If that was the level of the discussion, the Abbot might have led a trump. Let declarer try to make it then!

Over the next few rounds the Abbot picked up some good results against less skilled members of the novitiate. In general, however, he was quite impressed by the standard of play. Maybe, in twenty or thirty years' time, some of these fledgling performers would be capable of replacing the grandmasters currently in the monastery first team. It was not impossible.

The Abbot sighed as he took his seat against Brother Gavin and Brother Darryl. They had been playing for over a year now but were still totally hopeless. Anyone with so little natural ability should give up the game, really. Nothing could be gained by struggling on, week after week, like fish out of water.

'How are you two doing?' asked the Abbot, in an unsympathetic tone.

'Not very well,' the somewhat overweight Brother Gavin replied. 'We did have one good board when I made a 3NT.' He looked at his partner. 'That was above average, wasn't it?'

Brother Darryl studied his scorecard closely. 'Yes, I marked it as AV+. Mind you, we could do with a few more boards like that.'

Not on this particular round, I'm afraid, thought the Abbot as he drew his cards from the board. This was the lay-out:

Neither Vul.
Dealer South

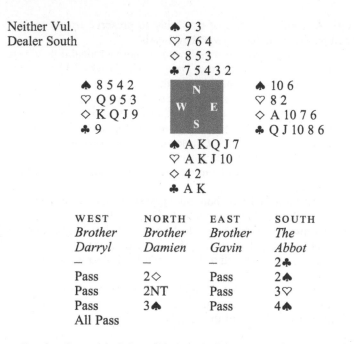

```
                              ♠ 9 3
                              ♡ 7 6 4
                              ◇ 8 5 3
                              ♣ 7 5 4 3 2
        ♠ 8 5 4 2                             ♠ 10 6
        ♡ Q 9 5 3                             ♡ 8 2
        ◇ K Q J 9                             ◇ A 10 7 6
        ♣ 9                                   ♣ Q J 10 8 6
                              ♠ A K Q J 7
                              ♡ A K J 10
                              ◇ 4 2
                              ♣ A K
```

WEST	NORTH	EAST	SOUTH
Brother	*Brother*	*Brother*	*The*
Darryl	*Damien*	*Gavin*	*Abbot*
—	—	—	2♣
Pass	2◇	Pass	2♠
Pass	2NT	Pass	3♡
Pass	3♠	Pass	4♠
All Pass			

Brother Darryl led the ◇K and continued with the ◇Q. The Abbot ruffed the third round of diamonds and paused to consider his prospects. If he drew trumps and found them 4-2, he would go down if the defender who won with the ♡Q had one or more diamonds to cash. Surely the best plan was to give up the first round of hearts. With any luck, a diamond continuation would then cause no harm; he would be able to ruff with dummy's ♠9. If it turned out that the ♡Q was doubleton and he had surrendered a cold overtrick with his expert line of play, so be it.

At Trick 4 the Abbot led the ♡10 from his hand. Brother Darryl played low and the ten won the trick. The Abbot then drew trumps in four rounds and cashed the two top clubs. He had to lose a trick to the ♡Q at the end, but ten tricks were his.

Brother Darryl turned towards the Abbot. 'That's a coincidence,' he said. 'I was reading about this type of hand only a few days ago. It was mentioned in a book that Brother Cameron lent me.'

The Abbot nodded, happy that his card play had been appreciated. 'Yes, it was an interesting one,' he replied.

'The book said the odds are 1700-to-1 against a nine-high hand,' continued Brother Darryl. 'It's called a yarborough.'

The Abbot sat back in his chair. No wonder this pair never

improved! A wondrous piece of card play to preserve trump control, and it had passed completely over their heads.

'Many years ago, players were allowed to claim a redeal if they were dealt a yarborough,' added Brother Darryl. 'That's why I like reading bridge books. You learn so much about the game.'

A few rounds later the Abbot faced Brother Sam and Brother Dwayne, both of whom had entered the novitiate only a few months before. Against such inexperienced opponents top scores were a near certainty. Still, it was good to see these young boys having a go. A few encouraging words might not go amiss.

The Abbot attempted a welcoming smile. 'How have you two been doing?' he asked.

'We scored the usual two bottoms against Brother Cameron,' the shaven-headed Brother Dwayne replied. 'He's brilliant.'

'Don't let him intimidate you,' declared the Abbot. 'He may think he's good but he rarely does well in the senior duplicate.'

'He told us he came second to Lucius and Paulo last week,' Brother Dwayne replied.

'I doubt it,' said the Abbot. 'I rarely look at the results but Brother Cameron played very poorly at my table.'

This was the next board of the round:

East-West Vul.
Dealer West

```
                    ♠ 10 8 6 5 3
                    ♡ 6 2
                    ◇ 10 8 3
                    ♣ K 9 3
   ♠ Q 4                              ♠ J 9 7 2
   ♡ 8 7             N                ♡ K J 4
   ◇ Q J 9 7       W   E              ◇ 6 4
   ♣ A Q J 7 4       S                ♣ 10 8 6 2
                    ♠ A K
                    ♡ A Q 10 9 5 3
                    ◇ A K 5 2
                    ♣ 5
```

WEST	NORTH	EAST	SOUTH
The	*Brother*	*Brother*	*Brother*
Abbot	*Sam*	*Damien*	*Dwayne*
1♣	Pass	2♣	4♡
All Pass			

The Abbot led the ◇Q against the heart game and Brother Dwayne won with the king. He had one loser in clubs and, after the opening lead, could presumably restrict his diamond losers to one by leading towards dummy's ◇10. In that case he needed to lose only one trump trick. Perhaps he should lead the ace of trumps, just in case an honour fell. If two spot cards appeared, he would have to guess whether the king was then bare and could be dropped, or the jack was bare and could be pinned by leading the queen. In his time as captain of bridge at the Holy Cross school in Chelmsford, he had usually played to pin the jack. It looked so much more impressive when it worked!

Another possibility occurred to the young player. The Abbot was likely to hold the ♣A. Suppose he played a club towards the king. The Abbot was unlikely to duck, after his partner had raised the suit, but he might have some difficulty in finding a safe return.

With this play in mind, Brother Dwayne cashed the ace and king of spades, happy to see the queen fall from the Abbot on the second round. There was a good chance that he would now be out of spades. When the novice continued with a low club, the Abbot rose with the ace and sat back in his chair. It was typical of his luck that a complete beginner at the game should exceed his brief at this particular moment. What could he do? A continuation in either minor was decidedly unattractive. It looked as if he would have to open the trump suit.

When the Abbot led the ♡8 to his partner's jack, Brother Dwayne won with the queen. He cashed the ace of trumps and both defenders followed, the king not appearing. A subsequent lead towards dummy's ◇10 then gave him the game.

Brother Damien glanced at the score-sheet on his right, seeing that -620 had not exactly given them a good score. Perhaps the Abbot should have led the ♣A after the suit had been raised. If he found the safe exit of a spade at Trick 2, declarer would have to read the cards well to escape for one down.

Brother Dwayne turned towards the Abbot. 'I played the two top spades so that you couldn't exit in that suit,' he said.

The Abbot blinked in disbelief at this inappropriate lack of modesty. 'It's not the St Titus way to gloat over a fortunate result,' he reprimanded. 'One day, if you're lucky, you will have the chance to play in the senior duplicate. On this deal almost the entire field would find the obvious play of cashing the top spades.'

With some difficulty Brother Damien managed to keep a straight face. What an absurd observation, even by the Abbot's standards! Cashing the spades had been a great play.

The penultimate round of the event saw the arrival of Brother Cameron, the regular partner of Brother Damien.

'Doing OK without me?' enquired Brother Damien.

'A few bidding misunderstandings,' Brother Cameron replied. He glanced down at his scorecard. 'Four tops over, maybe. How about you?'

'Shall we play the next board?' intervened the Abbot. 'Idle chat is best left till after the session.'

The players leaned forward to draw these cards:

```
Both Vul.              ♠ K Q J 9 2
Dealer South           ♡ 10 2
                       ◇ A 9 6
                       ♣ 8 5 3
         ♠ 8 6            N          ♠ 7 4 3
         ♡ K 7 5                     ♡ Q 8 6 4 3
         ◇ K 10 4 3    W     E       ◇ Q 8 7 2
         ♣ A 10 9 7      S           ♣ 2
                       ♠ A 10 5
                       ♡ A J 9
                       ◇ J 5
                       ♣ K Q J 6 4
```

WEST	NORTH	EAST	SOUTH
Brother	*Brother*	*Brother*	*The*
Cameron	*Damien*	*Mark*	*Abbot*
–	–	–	1NT
Pass	2♡	Pass	2♠
Pass	3NT	Pass	4♠
All Pass			

Brother Cameron led a trump and down went the dummy. The Abbot paused to assess his prospects. Ten tricks would be easy. To score well, he would need to set up the clubs for a discard or two. 'Nine, please,' he said. 'And a low club.'

The Abbot played the ♣K from his hand and this was allowed to win. It was possible from Brother Cameron's viewpoint that East had only one club. After ♣A and a club ruff, however, declarer would have a discard of dummy's heart loser. He would score five trumps, three clubs and the two red aces. The Abbot continued with the ♠A and the ♠10 to dummy's ♠K. 'Another low club,' he said.

The Abbot raised an eyebrow when East showed out on this trick, discarding a heart. That was unfortunate. He played the ♣Q from his hand and Brother Cameron held up the ace once again. The contract could no longer be made.

The Abbot tried the ♡J from hand but East won this trick and returned a heart. After a few seconds the Abbot rose with the ace, conceding one down. 'You had the ♡K?' he asked,

Brother Cameron nodded and the Abbot returned his cards to the board. At least he had avoided the ignominy of going two down.

Brother Cameron and Brother Damien shared a glance. Surely the contract should have been made? If the Abbot wanted to set up the clubs before drawing trumps, he should have left himself with a trump entry to his hand before playing the second round of clubs.

Brother Damien entered a '100' into the virgin East-West column and proffered the score-sheet for inspection. The Abbot waved it aside as if it were some troublesome insect. It could hardly be more obvious that no other West in this field would find the winning defence of holding up the ♣A twice. He suddenly felt extremely tired. There was no good reason why he should submit himself to these tortuous sessions in the novitiate, particularly after a full day's work. Next time he would ask Brother Xavier to perform the task. He made a note to that effect on the back of his scorecard. Yes, let's see how much he enjoyed it!

5. Eileen Wishbone's Obvious Raise

'Who are you playing in your National Inter-Club Knockout match tonight, Abbot?' asked Brother Aelred, as they met outside the monastery chapel. 'Anyone good?'

'I don't expect so,' replied the Abbot. 'Mr and Mrs Wishbone, Mr and Mrs Bowles. Need I say more?'

'Am I supposed to have heard of them?' asked Brother Aelred.

'No-one in the world has heard of them,' declared the Abbot. 'One could hardly wish for an easier draw than two married couples. If previous experience is anything to go by, they're probably fairly old too.'

'I'm not sure you're allowed to use the word 'old' any more,' said Brother Aelred. 'It's what the government calls ageist. To avoid implying any prejudice you have to look for a more kindly term.'

The Abbot had no time for such niceties of the modern age. 'Is that so?' he exclaimed. 'What is the approved term nowadays?'

'I'm not absolutely sure,' Brother Aelred replied. 'It could be geriatically challenged. Something like that, anyway.'

The appointed day soon arrived and the two couples, who were indeed somewhat elderly, were shown into the monastery cardroom. The Abbot nodded approvingly at the display of infirmity before him. 'May I take your coats?' he asked.

'I think I'll keep mine on, if you don't mind,' replied Eileen Wishbone. 'I don't know why, I'm feeling a bit chilly tonight.'

'Me too,' declared Adeline Bowles, looking round the high-ceilinged cardroom. 'It must be all this stonework that makes it so cold. Bill and I have central heating in our house.'

'I'm afraid that would be way beyond our financial means,' declared the Abbot. 'Every penny we earn goes on charitable work.'

Cecil Wishbone came to his wife's support. 'I dare say but it's unusually cold in here,' he said 'Perhaps you could have someone make up a fire in the fireplace over there.'

The Abbot had rarely encountered such rude opponents. Was querying the proffered hospitality part of good bridge ethics? Not as he saw it. 'I'll see what can be done at half-time,' he replied.

This was an early deal at the Abbot's table.

Both Vul.
Dealer West

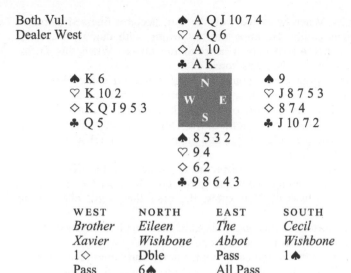

```
                    ♠ A Q J 10 7 4
                    ♡ A Q 6
                    ◇ A 10
                    ♣ A K
    ♠ K 6              N              ♠ 9
    ♡ K 10 2                          ♡ J 8 7 5 3
    ◇ K Q J 9 5 3   W    E            ◇ 8 7 4
    ♣ Q 5                             ♣ J 10 7 2
                       S
                    ♠ 8 5 3 2
                    ♡ 9 4
                    ◇ 6 2
                    ♣ 9 8 6 4 3
```

WEST	NORTH	EAST	SOUTH
Brother	*Eileen*	*The*	*Cecil*
Xavier	*Wishbone*	*Abbot*	*Wishbone*
1◇	Dble	Pass	1♠
Pass	6♠	All Pass	

Brother Xavier led the ◇K against the small slam in spades and down went the dummy.

'I couldn't believe it when this man opened the bidding,' Eileen Wishbone informed her husband. 'I was going to open Two Clubs.'

The Abbot stared at the dummy in disbelief. The old dear had bid Six Spades with four losers in her hand! Where on earth did she think three of those were going? It was typical of these weak players to overbid on good hands and underbid on bad hands.

The white-haired declarer did not look any more impressed with the dummy than the Abbot had been. 'Win with the ◇A, will you?' he said.

It seemed to Cecil Wishbone that his only chance of a make was to find a singleton ♠K. If he could drop that card under the ace, he would be able to cross to the ♠8 and take a heart finesse. In fact, if clubs were 3-3 he might be able to ruff the clubs good. Yes, he had two entries to his hand in the trump suit. He should be able to combine the two chances!

'Play the ♣A, please, Eileen,' said the declarer. 'And the ♣K.'

The ♣Q fell from West, making it somewhat unlikely that the club suit would break 3-3. He was about to cash the ♠A when an interesting idea occurred to him. If West's ♣Q was to be believed, he had no cards left in the suit. In that case a diamond exit might work well. 'Try the ◇10,' said Cecil Wishbone.

Brother Xavier won with the ◇J, the Abbot playing upwards to show three cards in the suit, and saw that he would have to open one of the major suits. When he exited with the ♠6, declarer finessed dummy's queen successfully. He drew the last trump with dummy's ace and crossed to his ♠5 to play a heart to the queen. When this finesse succeeded too, the slam was home.

'I was hoping clubs would be 3-3,' observed Cecil Wishbone. 'Rather a long shot once the queen fell on the second round.'

The Abbot surveyed his opponent disdainfully. If clubs had been 3-3, the slam would have gone down. Declarer's only chance was to find West with a doubleton club and then end-play him. Unless the ♠K was singleton, of course.

Eileen Wishbone turned suspiciously towards Brother Xavier. 'Did you have an opening bid?' she enquired. 'It wasn't one of those psyching bids, was it? You know, the ones that aren't allowed any more.'

'I had fourteen points and a six-card suit,' replied Brother Xavier, fanning his cards. 'A respectable opening in every way.'

At the other end of the card-room, Lucius and Paulo faced William Bowles, a long-retired accountant, and his somewhat frail wife, Adeline. This hand had just been dealt:

North-South Vul.
Dealer South

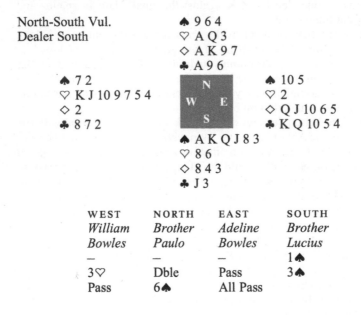

```
                    ♠ 9 6 4
                    ♡ A Q 3
                    ◇ A K 9 7
                    ♣ A 9 6
♠ 7 2                               ♠ 10 5
♡ K J 10 9 7 5 4         N          ♡ 2
◇ 2                  W       E      ◇ Q J 10 6 5
♣ 8 7 2                  S          ♣ K Q 10 5 4
                    ♠ A K Q J 8 3
                    ♡ 8 6
                    ◇ 8 4 3
                    ♣ J 3
```

WEST	NORTH	EAST	SOUTH
William	*Brother*	*Adeline*	*Brother*
Bowles	*Paulo*	*Bowles*	*Lucius*
–	–	–	1♠
3♡	Dble	Pass	3♠
Pass	6♠	All Pass	

The balding William Bowles led the ◇2. 'I hope this isn't too much,' said Brother Paulo, as he laid out the dummy.

Lucius won with the ◇A and drew trumps. There were eleven top tricks, assuming the heart finesse was right. West guarded the hearts and East was a huge favourite to guard the diamonds. Could he arrange a double squeeze with clubs as the pivot suit? Dummy's ♡3 would be the single threat against West, his own ◇8 would be the single threat against East; no-one could then keep a club guard. The trouble was that he needed to rectify the count. This could only be done by ducking a club and a second round of clubs would then remove dummy's ♣A, killing the entry in the pivot suit.

Another line of play occurred to Brother Lucius. If East did hold the ♣K and ♣Q, she could be caught in a simple squeeze in the minors. Playing for this ending instead, it would be possible to rectify the count in hearts. West's opening lead of the ◇2 was surely a singleton. In that case he would not be able to destroy dummy's diamond entry when he won the third round of hearts.

Adeline Bowles cast a disapproving eye over the declarer. Was he trying to freeze her to death? Not content with holding the match in the equivalent of a walk-in deep freeze, it seemed that these monks were going to spend ages playing every hand.

'Sorry to be so slow,' said Brother Lucius. Moving into action, he finessed the ♡Q successfully and cashed the ♡A, East showing out. He then called for the ♡3, discarding a diamond from his hand. West won the trick and exited with a club, taken with dummy's ace. With the ♣J now a threat against East, Brother Lucius ran his remaining trumps to reach this ending:

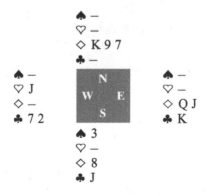

When the last trump was led, East had to throw one of her minor-suit guards. Since the diamond threat was before her eyes in the dummy, Mrs Bowles discarded the ♣K. Lucius then scored the last two tricks with the ♣J and dummy's ◇K.

'A club lead would have been nice, Bill,' Mrs Bowles observed. 'I had the king-queen sitting over dummy's ace.'

William Bowles turned towards Brother Lucius. 'Does a club lead make any difference?' he asked.

Lucius smiled at his opponent. 'It's not enough on its own,' he replied. 'I would duck the trick to your partner's queen and your wife would then have to find the ♣K return.'

'I would have done,' said Mrs Bowles firmly. 'I always return partner's suit.'

Back on the other table, the Abbot was finding the going tougher than he had expected. A few part-score deals had gone satisfactorily but he had yet to record anything approaching a big swing in the right direction. This was the last deal of the first half:

East-West Vul.
Dealer South

```
                    ♠ J 10 5
                    ♡ 5 2
                    ◇ 8 5 3 2
                    ♣ 10 8 7 2
    ♠ 7                              ♠ Q 9 6 4 3 2
    ♡ A K Q J 10 9 8 7 4    N        ♡ 6 3
    ◇ 10                  W   E      ◇ K Q J 9 4
    ♣ 9 5                   S        ♣ —
                    ♠ A K 8
                    ♡ —
                    ◇ A 7 6
                    ♣ A K Q J 6 4 3
```

WEST	NORTH	EAST	SOUTH
Brother	*Eileen*	*The*	*Cecil*
Xavier	*Wishbone*	*Abbot*	*Wishbone*
–	–	–	2♣
4♡	Pass	Pass	5♣
Pass	6♣	All Pass	

Mr and Mrs Wishbone bid to a small slam in clubs and Brother Xavier led the ♡K. He and the Abbot played 'ace for attitude, king for count', so the king lead requested a count signal. Down went the dummy and, as on the previous slam deal, three pairs of eyes stared at its contents in disbelief.

'Four nice trumps for you and a ruffing value,' Mrs Wishbone declared. 'It was an obvious raise.'

Her husband maintained an impassive expression. Commendable as it was for Eileen to express confidence in his cardplay, surely she should draw a limit somewhere?

The ♡2 was played from the dummy and the Abbot showed his count by playing the ♡6. Cecil Wishbone ruffed in his hand and drew trumps in two rounds with the ace and ten. After running the ♠J successfully, he cashed the ace and king of the suit. He then paused to consider his continuation. If West held king-queen doubleton in the diamond suit, he could ruff dummy's last heart and end-play West on the second round of diamonds. With only hearts left in his hand, he would have to give a ruff-and-discard. Yes, slim as it was, that seemed to be the best chance. This was the position as Cecil Wishbone led the ♢A:

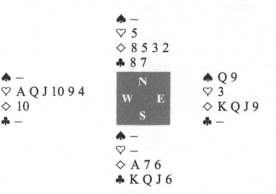

```
                    ♠ —
                    ♡ 5
                    ♢ 8 5 3 2
                    ♣ 8 7
    ♠ —                          ♠ Q 9
    ♡ A Q J 10 9 4               ♡ 3
    ♢ 10                         ♢ K Q J 9
    ♣ —                          ♣ —
                    ♠ —
                    ♡ —
                    ♢ A 7 6
                    ♣ K Q J 6
```

The ♢A drew only a disappointing ♢10 from West. Mr Wishbone did not like the look of this card. The opponents were competent players and if West had started with ♢K-10 he would surely have unblocked the king on the first round. In that case there was only one other line to try.

The elderly declarer crossed to dummy's ♣8 and called for the ♡5. The Abbot followed impotently with the ♡3 and declarer discarded a diamond. Brother Xavier had to win in the West seat and the enforced heart return conceded a ruff-and-discard. Declarer ruffed with dummy's last trump and, with an exaggerated flourish, threw the remaining diamond loser from his hand. The slam had been made.

'I thought it would be there,' declared Mrs Wishbone. 'I didn't like to pass Five Clubs with four-card trump support.'

Brother Xavier delivered an anguished look across the table. 'You needed to retain the ♡6 at Trick 1, Abbot,' he said. 'I can keep the ♡4 over here and that prevents the throw-in.'

'May I?' asked Mrs Wishbone, leaning to her right to inspect Brother Xavier's hand. 'There's a nine-card heart suit here, Cecil. I expect Adeline and Bill will sacrifice in Six Hearts. How many off does that go?'

'Only one off, I think,' her husband replied. 'Ah, the other table has finished too. I'll be quite interested to see what happened on those two slam deals.'

Two novices had been assigned to deliver the half-time pot of tea and the regulation margarine sandwiches. Brother Adam placed the over-sized teapot on the Abbot's table, trying to sneak a glance at his scorecard. For some reason the Abbot was covering it with his hand. 'Is the match going well, Abbot?' the novice enquired.

'These tea cups aren't very clean,' the Abbot replied. He reached for a white handkerchief and wiped the inside of his cup. 'I trust that you gave our visitors some clean crockery.'

The two novices left the cardroom together and Brother Damien caught his colleague's eye. 'Nineteen down at half-time!' he said. 'The Abbot won't want to lose to a team like that.'

'I thought he must be losing,' replied an amused Brother Adam.

'The two old couples were really chuffed about it,' Brother Damien continued. 'They didn't even complain about the sandwiches!'

6.   The Abbot Lowers His Sights

At half-time in their first-round National Inter-Club Knockout match, the monastery team found themselves 19 IMPs adrift. 'How can we possibly be losing to two married couples?' demanded the Abbot. 'Add their ages together and you wouldn't get much change from three hundred.'

Brother Paulo looked down at his score-card. Things had gone well at his table and he had expected a healthy lead. 'Don't worry, Abbot,' he replied. 'I will make sure they are put under maximum pressure in the second half.'

'Oh yes, that's just what we need,' said the Abbot heavily. 'Foolish overbidding into no-play games and slams? Yes, that will really put them under pressure.'

Two novices re-appeared to clear away the plates and tea cups. The margarine sandwiches had not proved popular on the visitors' table but they would be gratefully devoured in the novitiate. The second half began and this was an early board:

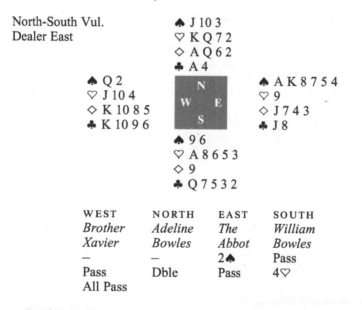

North-South Vul.
Dealer East

♠ J 10 3
♡ K Q 7 2
◇ A Q 6 2
♣ A 4

♠ Q 2
♡ J 10 4
◇ K 10 8 5
♣ K 10 9 6

♠ A K 8 7 5 4
♡ 9
◇ J 7 4 3
♣ J 8

♠ 9 6
♡ A 8 6 5 3
◇ 9
♣ Q 7 5 3 2

WEST	NORTH	EAST	SOUTH
Brother	*Adeline*	*The*	*William*
Xavier	*Bowles*	*Abbot*	*Bowles*
–	–	2♠	Pass
Pass	Dble	Pass	4♡
All Pass			

Brother Xavier led the ♠Q, winning the first trick, and continued with another spade to the Abbot's king. The Abbot usually took his time in defence but here it was totally obvious to continue with the ♠A. This would force the declarer and maybe promote a trump trick for Brother Xavier.

When the ♠A appeared on the table William Bowles ruffed with the ace, noting the diamond discard on his left. He finessed the ◇Q successfully and, without cashing the ◇A, ruffed a low diamond in his hand. A trump to the king allowed him to ruff dummy's remaining low diamond. He then returned to dummy with the ♡Q, East showing out. These cards were still to be played:

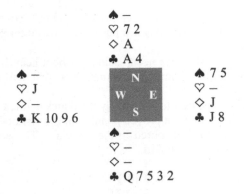

'Ace of diamonds, please,' said the bald-headed declarer.

Brother Xavier, sitting West, did not like the look of the situation. If he ruffed the ◇A he would have to lead a club, which would give away the contract if South held the ♣Q. He decided to mark time by discarding a club instead.

'Play a trump, please, Adeline,' said the declarer.

Brother Xavier was thrown on lead and now had no alternative but to lead a club from the king. William Bowles ran this successfully to his queen and claimed the contract.

'Well done, Bill,' said the comely Mrs Bowles. 'You didn't have very much there, did you?'

'Enough,' her husband replied. 'It was bound to play well with two five-timers.'

The Abbot thought back over the play. The old boy had timed it very competently, it seemed. If he had cashed the ◇A prematurely, before taking the two diamond ruffs, West could have overruffed the fourth round of diamonds and exited safely with a trump.

'Difficult one for you, Abbot,' said Brother Xavier.

The Abbot groaned inwardly. What was he supposed to have done now? After promoting a trump trick for Xavier, there had been nothing for him to do.

'It looked right, playing a third top spade,' continued Brother Xavier, 'but I don't think he can do it if you play a trump instead.'

'He can follow the same line, can't he?' protested the Abbot. 'He wins in the dummy, ruffs a spade with the ace, finesses the diamond, ruffs a diamond and so on.'

'I think you'll find that he ends in the wrong hand,' said Brother Xavier. 'He would end in the South hand with no trumps left and no way to throw me on lead.'

The Abbot beckoned for the next board to be brought into position. Xavier's analysis was notoriously unreliable. In any case, it had been totally obvious to play a third high spade. No player in the entire universe would have defended differently.

At the other side of the cardroom, Lucius and Paulo faced Eileen and Cecil Wishbone. These four hands had just been dealt:

```
Both Vul.                  ♠ 6 4
Dealer North               ♡ 10 3
                           ◇ Q 7
                           ♣ A K Q 10 8 7 2
         ♠ Q J 10 8 2            N            ♠ 3
         ♡ 9 7 5 4                            ♡ A K J 8 2
         ◇ J 2          W            E        ◇ K 10 9 6 5
         ♣ J 4                               ♣ 9 5
                               S
                           ♠ A K 9 7 5
                           ♡ Q 6
                           ◇ A 8 4 3
                           ♣ 6 3
```

WEST	NORTH	EAST	SOUTH
Eileen	*Brother*	*Cecil*	*Brother*
Wishbone	*Paulo*	*Wishbone*	*Lucius*
–	3NT	Pass	5♣
All Pass			

Paulo opened with a Gambling 3NT and Lucius responded Five Clubs, hoping that an eleventh trick would materialize from somewhere. There was no further bidding and West led the ♠Q. Lucius won with the ace and saw that the contract would be an easy make if spades broke 3-3. After drawing trumps, he could establish the spades with a ruff and return to enjoy them with the ♢A.

Brother Lucius drew trumps in two rounds and decided to play a few more rounds before trying to set up his spade suit. To encourage West to discard spades, he threw the spade nine on the third round of trumps. He was pleased to see West throw a spade on this trick too. It would now be possible to ruff the spades good even if West had started with four cards in the suit.

On the next three rounds of trumps, Lucius discarded two diamonds and a heart. No more spade discards were forthcoming and he now had to test the situation in the spade suit. 'Play the ♠6, please,' said Brother Lucius.

Bad news arrived when East discarded on this trick. Lucius won with the ♠K and surveyed this end position:

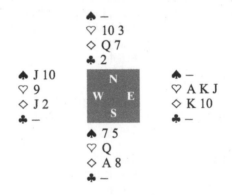

```
                    ♠ —
                    ♡ 10 3
                    ◇ Q 7
                    ♣ 2
        ♠ J 10                      ♠ —
        ♡ 9           N             ♡ A K J
        ◇ J 2      W     E          ◇ K 10
        ♣ —           S             ♣ —
                    ♠ 7 5
                    ♡ Q
                    ◇ A 8
                    ♣ —
```

The only remaining hope was an end-play on East. Lucius ruffed a spade in the dummy, his hopes rising as East spent some time considering his discard. Eventually Cecil Wishbone threw the ♡A. 'Low heart, please,' said Brother Lucius.

Hoping that his partner held the ♡Q, East contributed the ♡J on this trick. Declarer's bare queen won and the contract was made.

'Oh dear,' exclaimed Mrs Wishbone. 'What happened there, Cecil?'

'There was nothing I could do,' her husband replied. 'If I keep the ace and king of hearts, I'm thrown in and have to lead away from the ◇K.'

'There must be some way to beat it,' persisted Mrs Wishbone.

'Lead a red suit and you break up the end-play,' Cecil Wishbone replied. 'Not that you're likely to with that spade holding.'

Back on the other table, the Abbot was not enjoying himself. Two elderly married couples had no right to play the cards so well. If someone had been good enough to inform him that the opponents were reasonable players, he would have taken more trouble with his match preparations. For a start he would have gone to bed earlier. It wasn't as if the late-night football had been any good. Drab 1-0 wins for Middlesbrough and Aston Villa in the Carling Cup? It was hardly worth crashing out of this national knock-out event to witness that sort of fare.

The players drew their cards for this board:

East-West Vul.
Dealer South

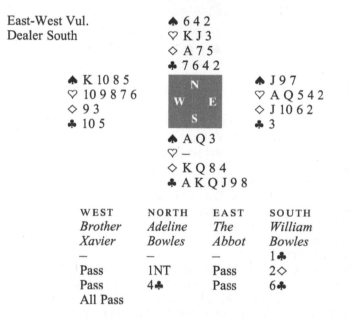

```
              ♠ 6 4 2
              ♡ K J 3
              ◇ A 7 5
              ♣ 7 6 4 2
♠ K 10 8 5                    ♠ J 9 7
♡ 10 9 8 7 6       N         ♡ A Q 5 4 2
◇ 9 3          W     E        ◇ J 10 6 2
♣ 10 5             S          ♣ 3
              ♠ A Q 3
              ♡ –
              ◇ K Q 8 4
              ♣ A K Q J 9 8
```

WEST	NORTH	EAST	SOUTH
Brother	*Adeline*	*The*	*William*
Xavier	*Bowles*	*Abbot*	*Bowles*
–	–	–	1♣
Pass	1NT	Pass	2◇
Pass	4♣	Pass	6♣
All Pass			

Mr and Mrs Bowles bid to a small slam in clubs and Brother Xavier led the ♡10. When dummy appeared, the monastery players exchanged a glance. The jump to 4♣ had been imaginative, to put it politely. With the heart honours an unknown quantity, even Brother Paulo might have baulked at such a forward move.

'Cover with the jack, will you?' said William Bowles.

The Abbot played the ♡Q and declarer ruffed. After drawing trumps in two rounds, he cashed the ◇K and ◇A. 'King of hearts, please,' he said.

The Abbot covered once more, with the ace, and declarer ruffed. All would be well if the diamonds broke 3-3 but West showed out when William Bowles cashed the ♢Q. A diamond ruff returned the lead to the dummy and these cards remained:

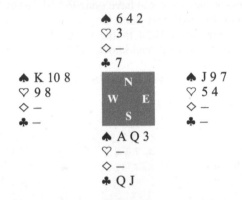

```
                    ♠ 6 4 2
                    ♡ 3
                    ♢ —
                    ♣ 7
   ♠ K 10 8                        ♠ J 9 7
   ♡ 9 8          N                ♡ 5 4
   ♢ —        W       E            ♢ —
   ♣ —            S                ♣ —
                    ♠ A Q 3
                    ♡ —
                    ♢ —
                    ♣ Q J
```

The obvious move at this stage was to take a spade finesse, making the contract if it succeeded. William Bowles had been watching the heart pips closely, however, and was fairly certain how that suit lay. 'Play the ♡3,' he said.

The Abbot followed with the ♡4 and declarer threw the ♠3, Brother Xavier winning the trick. A fourth round of hearts would concede a ruff-and-discard, so he was forced to open the spade suit. Declarer scored two tricks with his ace-queen and the slam was made.

'What happened in hearts?' cried the Abbot. 'Didn't you have a lower spot-card to keep?'

'I don't think so,' Brother Xavier replied. He retrieved his cards from the table and faced them for the Abbot's inspection. 'No, look, 10-9-8-7-6. If I'd had something like the 2, I would have kept it.'

William Bowles looked happily across the table. 'You pushed the boat out with your 4♣ call, Adeline,' he said.

'I could hardly bid just 3♣ with 4-card support,' his wife replied.

'Mind you,' Mr Bowles continued, 'the slam wouldn't be so easy on a minor-suit lead.'

The Abbot leaned forward. 'That's right,' he said. 'Without a heart lead he wouldn't have enough entries to dummy to ruff two hearts. Even if he did, he would try to end-play you with the king on the third round. That ♡10 lead gave him the slam on a plate.'

'My only alternative was a spade,' Brother Xavier replied. 'I don't see how I can lead a minor suit on that bidding.'

Not long afterwards the monastery team reconvened to compare scores. 'We had a couple of good ones,' said Brother Lucius. 'If you're all right, it should be enough.'

The Abbot's heart sank. A couple of good ones? What use was that? With the Wishbones playing so luckily at his own table, four or five good ones were needed.

The final comparison did indeed confirm the Abbot's suspicions. The visitors' half-time lead had been extended to 24 IMPs and the match was lost.

'Well, you made a good fight of it,' declared Eileen Wishbone, leaning heavily on her walking stick as the Abbot escorted his guests back to the main gate. 'Usually in the early rounds we win by 60 or 70. There's not much fun in that.'

'No, it was a very close game,' said Adeline Bowles. She turned to smile at the Abbot. 'It's embarrassing to admit it but we lost in the first round once. You get a free entry to the NICKO Plate.'

The Abbot pretended not to hear. NICKO Plate? A player of his eminence wouldn't be seen dead playing in a secondary event like that. Nor would it be fair to the other contestants for an all-expert team to enter.

'You still get green points in the Plate,' continued Adeline Bowles. 'I was surprised to hear that.'

The Abbot perked up at this news. Perhaps, after all, it was their duty to be good citizens and support the event. Brother Xavier could certainly do with the practice.

7. Brother Lucius's Underbid

The annual monastery pairs championship took place over two consecutive Thursdays in July. The current holders, as had been pointed out more than once during the past year, were the Abbot and Brother Xavier. Paulo had been away in Italy, visiting old colleagues, but the Abbot claimed that this had made no difference to the result. He had played at such a high level himself that few pairs in the country would have been able to keep pace.

'Good evening, Abbot,' said Brother Adam, taking his seat. 'You won this event last year, didn't you?'

The Abbot nodded happily. 'With Brother Xavier's assistance, of course,' he replied. One can't win these events single-handedly.'

'Brother Paulo was away, wasn't he?' queried Brother Stephen. 'It may be a bit more competitive this year.'

The Abbot tilted his head to one side. 'Not necessarily,' he replied. 'Overbidding consistently is hardly a winning strategy in a two-session pairs event.'

The players drew their cards for this board:

Neither Vul.
Dealer North

```
                    ♠ A 3 2
                    ♡ A K J 10 7
                    ◇ 8 4
                    ♣ K 7 6
      ♠ —                          ♠ J 8 7 6 4
      ♡ 9 8 6          N           ♡ 4 2
      ◇ K J 3      W       E       ◇ 10 9 5
      ♣ A Q J 10 8 5 4    S        ♣ 9 3 2
                    ♠ K Q 10 9 5
                    ♡ Q 5 3
                    ◇ A Q 7 6 2
                    ♣ —
```

WEST	NORTH	EAST	SOUTH
Brother	*Brother*	*Brother*	*The*
Adam	*Xavier*	*Stephen*	*Abbot*
–	1♡	Pass	1♠
3♣	Pass	Pass	3◇
Pass	4♠	Pass	6♠
All Pass			

The Abbot arrived in a slam and Brother Adam led the ♣A. The dummy was laid out and the Abbot gave every impression of liking what he saw. Five spades, five hearts and the ◇A gave him eleven tricks on top. After this foolish ♣A lead, dummy's ♣K would bring the total to twelve. How often had he instructed the novices not to lead unsupported aces? The board would be an instructive example to show to next week's class. The Abbot turned towards Brother Adam. 'Remind me to make a note of this deal at the end, will you?' he said.

The Abbot ruffed the club lead and played the king of trumps. He stopped in his tracks when West showed out. Could twelve tricks still be made? Dummy's hearts wouldn't be much use because East would be able to ruff at some stage and would still have one more trump than the dummy. It seemed that he would need to find a 3-3 diamond break, with East holding the king. Yes, he could then take a winning finesse and establish the diamonds with a ruff. When he subsequently ran the hearts, he could overruff East, draw all the trumps but one and throw the club loser from dummy. East could take his long trump whenever he wished. Dummy and the South hand would both be high.

The Abbot's masterful analysis was unproductive. When he crossed to dummy with a heart and took a diamond finesse, the queen lost to the king. He had to lose one more trick in the trump suit and the slam was one down.

The Abbot sighed. 'Trumps were 5-0,' he exclaimed.

Brother Xavier nodded sympathetically. 'It's no good if you discard at Trick 1, is it?' he asked. 'Perhaps you can win the return, play a trump to the ace and pick up East's trumps.'

The Abbot took his time in returning his cards to the wallet. Discard on the first trick? How incredibly annoying! Modest performer as Xavier was, it seemed that he might be right.

'I spotted that safety play the moment dummy went down,' the Abbot replied. 'I can hardly play that way at Pairs. I had thirteen tricks if the diamond finesse was working.'

Brother Adam leant forward. 'You asked me to remind you to take a note of the deal, Abbot,' he said.

'There's no time for that now,' grunted the Abbot. 'Let's get on with the next one.'

A few rounds later, the monastery's two top pairs faced each other. The Abbot peered over his glasses at Brother Paulo. 'I'm pleased to see you haven't fled from the battlefield on this occasion,' he declared. 'When we won the event a year ago, there were those who attributed the victory to your absence. Not that a final score of 9.41 tops above average left much room for doubt.'

This was the first board of the round:

North-South Vul.
Dealer North

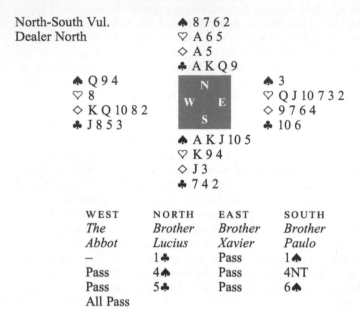

```
                    ♠ 8 7 6 2
                    ♡ A 6 5
                    ◇ A 5
                    ♣ A K Q 9
   ♠ Q 9 4                          ♠ 3
   ♡ 8              N               ♡ Q J 10 7 3 2
   ◇ K Q 10 8 2   W   E             ◇ 9 7 6 4
   ♣ J 8 5 3        S               ♣ 10 6
                    ♠ A K J 10 5
                    ♡ K 9 4
                    ◇ J 3
                    ♣ 7 4 2
```

WEST	NORTH	EAST	SOUTH
The	*Brother*	*Brother*	*Brother*
Abbot	*Lucius*	*Xavier*	*Paulo*
–	1♣	Pass	1♠
Pass	4♠	Pass	4NT
Pass	5♣	Pass	6♠
All Pass			

The Abbot led the ◇K and surveyed the dummy with a pained expression. No doubt Brother Paulo's Blackwood bid had been totally unsound. It was typical of his luck to find so many controls in the dummy.

Brother Paulo won with dummy's ◇A and played the two top trumps, discovering that he had a loser in the suit. The Abbot surveyed the scene contentedly. The 3-1 trump break was no more than Paulo deserved. He was a tolerable card-player, yes, but his bidding was hopelessly wild. His idea of discovering whether partner had the right cards for a slam was to leap to the six-level and wait until dummy went down. What an attitude!

Brother Paulo cashed the ace and king of clubs, noting with interest the fall of the ♣10 from East. It seemed to him that he needed West to hold four clubs. He returned to his hand with the ♡K and led a third round of clubs. 'Play the nine,' he said.

The finesse succeeded and he continued with the ♣Q, throwing his losing diamond. A diamond ruff returned the lead to the South hand and these cards remained:

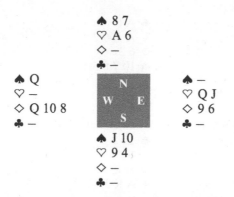

```
                    ♠ 8 7
                    ♡ A 6
                    ◇ —
                    ♣ —
      ♠ Q              N              ♠ —
      ♡ —                             ♡ Q J
      ◇ Q 10 8    W         E         ◇ 9 6
      ♣ —              S              ♣ —
                    ♠ J 10
                    ♡ 9 4
                    ◇ —
                    ♣ —
```

When a heart was led towards dummy, the Abbot could see little point in ruffing with his master trump. He discarded a diamond and dummy's ♡A won the trick. A third round of trumps end-played the Abbot and the ensuing ruff-and-discard allowed Brother Paulo to dispose of his heart loser. Twelve tricks had been made.

'Incredibly fortunate lie of the cards!' exclaimed the Abbot. 'And what was this Blackwood bid with two losing diamonds in your hand? Have you never heard of cue-bidding?'

'Such good trumps and an outside king,' the Italian replied. 'I felt sure there would be a play for it.'

'It's a bit more difficult if you lead your singleton heart, Abbot,' said Brother Xavier. 'If he starts with two rounds of trumps, he goes down wherever he wins the heart lead.'

'That's true,' said Brother Paulo. 'Say I win in my hand with the ♡K. To make the contract I have to play ace of trumps, two top clubs and a trump to the king. Yes, then I can finesse in clubs and I'm back on the original line.'

'I don't see how else you can play it,' said the Abbot. 'It seems the obvious line on a heart lead.'

This was the second board of the round:

East-West Vul.
Dealer South

```
                        ♠ A 6
                        ♡ A K 9 7 4
                        ◇ 6 3
                        ♣ 10 7 6 5
    ♠ Q J 7 5 4 3              ♠ K 9 2
    ♡ 10 3           N         ♡ Q J 8 5 2
    ◇ 4           W    E       ◇ Q J 10 5 2
    ♣ Q 9 8 3        S         ♣ —
                        ♠ 10 8
                        ♡ 6
                        ◇ A K 9 8 7
                        ♣ A K J 4 2
```

WEST	NORTH	EAST	SOUTH
The	*Brother*	*Brother*	*Brother*
Abbot	*Lucius*	*Xavier*	*Paulo*
–	–	–	1◇
Pass	1♡	Pass	2♣
Pass	3♣	Pass	5♣
All Pass			

Lucius thought for some time over 5♣. His hand was a giant for the raise to 3♣. Also, with the ♠A in his hand it was possible they had bypassed a higher-scoring 3NT game. Perhaps he should bid a sixth club? Opposite any normal bidder he would have done, but Paulo had doubtless already allowed for him being maximum.

The Abbot, who had been willing Brother Lucius to bid on, was disappointed when the bidding died at the five-level. He led the ♠Q and down went the dummy. 'Hope this isn't too much,' said Brother Lucius.

Brother Paulo raised an eyebrow at the three top cards in the majors. If trumps were 2-2 he would probably make all thirteen tricks. It was unlike Lucius to take such a pessimistic view. He won the spade lead with dummy's ace and played a trump to the ace. When East showed out, Paulo cheered up considerably. 'What a lucky partner I have,' he exclaimed.

The Abbot winced. The one time in a decade that Lucius and Paulo underbid and, by some magic, they find everything breaking badly.

Brother Paulo played dummy's two top hearts, throwing his spade loser. He continued with the ace and king of diamonds, the Abbot ruffing the second round. Paulo ruffed the spade return and led a third round of diamonds. The Abbot discarded and he ruffed in the dummy.

When a third round of hearts was ruffed with the jack, the Abbot overruffed with the queen. He was on lead in this end position:

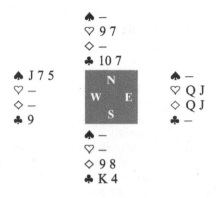

If the Abbot returned a spade, declarer would make the four remaining trumps separately on a cross-ruff. He therefore returned his last trump, covered by the ten in dummy.

Xavier paused to consider his discard, but Paulo had a complete count on the hand and knew that it would make no difference. He faced his remaining cards. 'You throw a heart, I let dummy's club ten win and ruff a heart good,' he said. You throw a diamond, I overtake with club king and ruff a diamond good.'

Xavier nodded. 'Pretty ending,' he said. 'A suicide seesaw squeeze if I'm not mistaken.'

'It just happened,' Brother Paulo replied modestly. 'I didn't do anything clever to set it up.'

He's right about that, thought the Abbot. A complete top for them, you could bet on it, just by sitting there. It was a pity someone couldn't invent a version of bridge where the ridiculous element of luck was excluded. Unlucky players such as himself would not then operate under such a handicap. Not that he disbelieved the Laws of Chance, it went without saying, but when was the last time he had grossly underbid a hand and been rescued by a bad trump break? The Great Dealer moved in mysterious ways, it was well known, but surely he should factor in some degree of fairness. That's what he would have done . . . had their roles been exchanged.

Part II Claude Yorke-Smith's Visit

8.   Brother Zac Reads the Cards

The Abbot's brother, Claude Yorke-Smith, was owner of a small hotel in the West Country. He regarded it as his privilege to visit the monastery whenever he wished. The lack of general comfort in his guest cell did not affect him unduly, since his Range Rover was easily big enough to accommodate a well-sprung mattress. With the BBC predicting a cold spell, he had also brought a duck-down duvet with him, a half-price bargain from Amazon.

'Give me a hand with this mattress, will you, Hugo?' said Claude Yorke-Smith. 'It's heavier than it looks.'

The Abbot beckoned for the assistance of Brother Cameron, who was walking nearby. There was no sense in putting his own back at risk. 'Would you like to watch at my table in the Charity Pairs tonight, Claude?' he asked. 'If not, we could probably find you a partner.'

'No need,' Claude replied. 'I don't mind playing with you.'

Later that evening, the Charity Pairs began:

Both Vul.
Dealer South

♠ K Q 9 2	
♡ 7 5	
◇ A 2	
♣ A 8 7 6 2	

West	East
♠ 8	♠ J 10 4
♡ A K J 6 4 3	♡ Q 10 9 2
◇ Q 10 6 4 3	◇ 9
♣ 9	♣ J 10 5 4 3

♠ A 7 6 5 3
♡ 8
◇ K J 8 7 5
♣ K Q

WEST	NORTH	EAST	SOUTH
Claude	*Brother*	*The*	*Brother*
Yorke-Smith	*Sextus*	*Abbot*	*Zac*
–	–	–	1♠
2♡	3♡	4♡	4♠
5♡	6♠	All Pass	

Claude Yorke-Smith led the ♡K and continued with the ♡A, ruffed by declarer. The Abbot was not overjoyed at this start to the play. Brother Sextus had a doubleton heart. Would he have ventured a slam without the 5♡ bid? In his eyes that had surely tipped the odds in favour of South holding a singleton heart.

Brother Zac drew trumps in three rounds. When he played the two club honours in his hand, West discarded a heart on the second round. He paused to assess the distribution of the defenders' hands. The Abbot had signalled an even count on the opening lead. Surely West's shape was 1-6-5-1. Only one trump remained in dummy, so how should he tackle the diamond suit?

Deciding that his best chance was to find that the Abbot's singleton was the 10 or 9, Brother Zac reached for the ◇J. This was covered by the queen and dummy's ace, the ◇9 appearing from East. He threw a diamond on the ♣A, returned to the ◇K and led the ◇8 for a ruffing finesse against West's ◇10. He then claimed the last two tricks with a club ruff and the established ◇7.

The Abbot thrust his cards back into the board. Thank goodness he wouldn't have to partner Claude again for a while. Much as he would dispute it, he made everything so easy for the opponents!

Not long afterwards, the Abbot and his brother faced a competent pair from the novitiate:

```
North-South Vul.        ♠ 9 4
Dealer East             ♡ Q 6 5
                        ◇ A Q 10 9 3
                        ♣ 7 5 3
    ♠ Q J 10 8 3 2              ♠ 6
    ♡ 10 9 3          N         ♡ K J 8 4
    ◇ 8 7 5      W       E      ◇ K 4 2
    ♣ 6              S          ♣ K J 10 9 4
                        ♠ A K 7 5
                        ♡ A 7 2
                        ◇ J 6
                        ♣ A Q 8 2
```

WEST	NORTH	EAST	SOUTH
Brother	*Claude*	*Brother*	*The*
Stephen	*Yorke-Smith*	*Adam*	*Abbot*
–	–	1♣	Dble
2♠	3◇	Pass	3NT
All Pass			

The pale-faced Brother Stephen placed the ♠Q on the table. 'These diamonds should be worth a few tricks,' observed Claude Yorke-Smith as he laid out the dummy.

The Abbot was unimpressed by what he saw. The ◇K was marked offside by the opening bid and Brother Adam was fully capable of holding up that card for one round. He won the spade lead with the king and ran the ◇J. Brother Adam surveyed the scene for a few seconds and decided to play low. The Abbot sighed. The declarers at many tables would have an easy ride, with East taking the king immediately. How could he retrieve the situation?

The Abbot continued with a diamond to the ace and exited with the ◇Q to East's king, throwing a spade. Brother Adam, who had no spade to return, switched to the ♣J. After finessing the ♣Q successfully, the Abbot turned his mind to an end-play on East. He cashed the ♣A, West showing out, and Brother Adam paused for a short while before contributing the ♣9 to this trick. The Abbot continued with his remaining spade honour, just in case East held another spade. These cards were still in play:

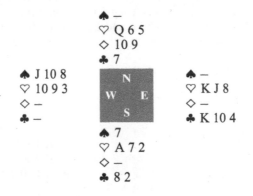

```
              ♠ —
              ♡ Q 6 5
              ◇ 10 9
              ♣ 7
♠ J 10 8                      ♠ —
♡ 10 9 3        N            ♡ K J 8
◇ —          W     E         ◇ —
♣ —             S            ♣ K 10 4
              ♠ 7
              ♡ A 7 2
              ◇ —
              ♣ 8 2
```

The Abbot extracted the ♣2 from his hand, intending to end-play East. After cashing three rounds of clubs, East would have to lead away from his marked ♡K. The Abbot would then score two heart tricks and one diamond for the contract. At the last moment, he reconsidered his play to this trick. Goodness me! If he made the mistake of leading the ♣2, East might have the wit to win with the ♣10 and return the ♣4 to declarer's bare ♣8. By sacrificing one trick in clubs, he would save two tricks from being end-played.

With the air of a multiple world champion, the Abbot returned the ♣2 to his hand and led the ♣8 instead. East had to win the trick or he would be thrown in on the next round of clubs. He cashed two further club tricks and then had to exit with a heart. The Abbot ran this to dummy's queen and triumphantly claimed the contract.

Claude Yorke-Smith, who had been fiddling with his mobile phone during the play, looked up. 'Was it there?' he asked.

The Abbot looked wearily across the table. 'Had you been following proceedings, you would have enjoyed a rather attractive end-play,' he replied.

'I can't afford to waste time at my age,' his brother replied. 'Mavis is holding the fort back at the hotel and she sent me an important email about a couple of late bookings.'

'It's not a good example to set these youngsters,' muttered the Abbot. 'Needless to say, mobile phones are banned in our community.'

A few rounds later, the Abbot faced his regular partner, Brother Xavier. With all the half-decent players already booked in for the Charity Pairs, Xavier had persuaded the occasional player, Brother Arbuthnot, to participate.

'Sorry for the late change of arrangements,' said the Abbot, as Xavier eased back the South seat. 'Not my fault, you realize. Anyway, how has the new partnership been faring?'

'Not too badly,' Brother Xavier replied. 'It's amazing how much can be done with just Stayman and Blackwood.'

'You're not playing transfer responses?' queried the Abbot.

The elderly Brother Arbuthnot leaned forward. 'The first time I tried them, my partner forgot and we scored a complete zero in a 3-2 fit. Never again!'

This was the first board of the round:

Both Vul.
Dealer South

```
                    ♠ 6 4 2
                    ♡ 7 5
                    ◇ A 6
                    ♣ K J 10 9 3 2
   ♠ J 7 5 3          N          ♠ Q 10 8
   ♡ Q 10 8 3     W       E      ♡ A 9 6 4
   ◇ 10 8 5 3                    ◇ K 9 2
   ♣ 5                 S          ♣ A 8 6
                    ♠ A K 9
                    ♡ K J 2
                    ◇ Q J 7 4
                    ♣ Q 7 4
```

WEST	NORTH	EAST	SOUTH
Claude	*Brother*	*The*	*Brother*
Yorke-Smith	*Arbuthnot*	*Abbot*	*Xavier*
–	–	–	1NT
Pass	3♣	Pass	3NT
All Pass			

Claude Yorke-Smith led the ♡3 and down went the dummy.

'I was hoping you'd bid that,' declared the white-haired Brother Arbuthnot. 'My club suit should be very useful in 3NT.'

The Abbot made no comment in the East seat. How truly hopeless these lesser players were! If Brother Arbuthnot thought his hand would make a good dummy in 3NT, why in Heaven's name had he not bid 3NT? It was hardly appropriate for him to point this out, but surely Brother Xavier would do so.

'Very nice dummy, partner,' said Brother Xavier. 'Thank you!'

The Abbot won the heart lead with the ace and turned his mind to the defence. Surely this was the right moment to return the ◇K. That would be a Merrimac Coup. Or was it a Deschapelles Coup? Either way, it would dislodge the ◇A and he could then hold up the ♣A to kill the dummy. Looking up to make sure that he had everyone's attention, the Abbot laid the ◇K on the table.

Brother Xavier acknowledged this play with a small nod. He won in dummy and called for the ♣J, which was allowed to win. When the ♣6 and ♣5 appeared on the trick, it was fairly obvious that clubs were 3-1. The defenders would be able to cut him off from dummy's club suit. What else could he try?

Brother Xavier could now count eight tricks. To increase this to nine, he would have to end-play West to give him a second heart trick. The first step was to play three rounds of spades without allowing East to gain the lead and switch back to hearts. 'Two of spades, please,' said Brother Xavier.

The Abbot inserted the ♠10 and Xavier won with the ace. He then played a low club to dummy's ten. West discarded a heart and the Abbot had to hold up his ace for a second time. 'And the ♠4,' requested Brother Xavier.

When the Abbot followed with the ♠8, Brother Xavier covered with his ♠9. West, the safe hand, won the trick and exited passively with a third round of spades to declarer's king. Xavier cashed the ◇Q and ◇J, leaving these cards still to be played:

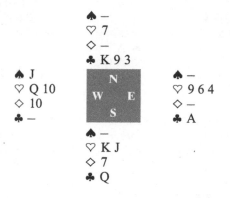

```
              ♠ —
              ♡ 7
              ◇ —
              ♣ K 9 3
  ♠ J                        ♠ —
  ♡ Q 10      N              ♡ 9 6 4
  ◇ 10     W     E           ◇ —
  ♣ —         S              ♣ A
              ♠ —
              ♡ K J
              ◇ 7
              ♣ Q
```

Brother Xavier exited with a diamond to West's ten. After cashing his spade winner, Claude Yorke-Smith had to return a heart into the ♡K-J and the game was made.

'Not the best, partner,' observed Claude Yorke-Smith. 'You gave him three diamond tricks.'

'The ◇K was an expert play to remove the entry to dummy,' retorted the Abbot. 'If I woodenly return a heart, he makes five clubs, two spades, the ♡K and the ◇A.'

'Anything's better than handing him the contract on a plate,' Claude replied. 'You wouldn't find me switching to the ◇K.'

There I can agree with you, thought the Abbot.

The session was nearly at an end when the Abbot and his brother faced Brother Lucius and Brother Paulo.

'Always good to see you here, Claude,' said Brother Lucius, moving into the South seat. 'Will you be with us for long?'

'Just a week or two,' Claude Yorke-Smith replied. 'My wife said she needed a bit of a rest.'

'A rest?' queried Brother Lucius. 'I'd have thought that running the hotel by herself would be quite an arduous business.'

Yorke-Smith smiled to himself. 'Women are hard to fathom at the best of times,' he replied. 'For some reason she says it's more stressful when I'm there to help her.'

The players drew their cards for this deal:

Neither Vul.
Dealer South

```
                      ♠ 9
                      ♡ 8 7 5 4
                      ◇ Q J 9 4
                      ♣ 8 6 3 2
   ♠ K Q J 10 5 4          N          ♠ 8 2
   ♡ 9                 W        E      ♡ K J 10 6 2
   ◇ 8 7 5 3               S          ◇ 10 6 2
   ♣ 10 5                              ♣ J 7 4
                      ♠ A 7 6 3
                      ♡ A Q 3
                      ◇ A K
                      ♣ A K Q 9
```

WEST	NORTH	EAST	SOUTH
Claude	*Brother*	*The*	*Brother*
Yorke-Smith	*Paulo*	*Abbot*	*Lucius*
–	–	–	2♣
3♠	Pass	Pass	3NT
All Pass			

The ♠K was led and Brother Lucius held up the ace on the first round. When spades were continued, he threw a club from dummy and won in his hand.

With no apparent entry to dummy, Brother Lucius turned his mind towards an end-play on East. He played four rounds of clubs, the other three hands discarding diamonds. The ◇A and ◇K came next, leaving these cards still to be played:

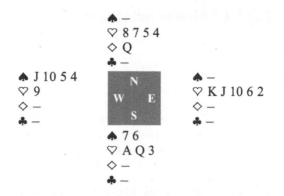

Brother Lucius had scored seven tricks and the ♡A was good for an eighth trick. West could be counted for an original 6-1-4-2 shape and Lucius now exited with the ♡Q, aiming to prevent West from winning the trick and cashing four spade winners. The ♡9 duly appeared from West and dummy followed with a low card.

The Abbot surveyed the scene with no great enthusiasm. If he won with the king, he would have to return the ♡J or ♡10 to prevent declarer running a low-card exit to the dummy. Declarer would then be able to win with the ace and lead his last card to dummy's ♡87. Not only would dummy score a heart trick subsequently, the ◇Q would be brought to life for an overtrick.

Although it pained him to do so, the Abbot allowed the ♡Q to win. Declarer had his ninth trick but he would at least be prevented from enjoying an overtrick. Brother Lucius cashed the ♡A and returned his remaining cards to the board, claiming nine tricks.

The Abbot could see that his brother was trying to work out what had happened near the end. 'I had to duck the ♡Q,' he informed him. 'He makes an overtrick otherwise.'

Claude Yorke-Smith leaned to his left, peering at the solid column of plus-scores for East-West. 'You seem to be the only East player to get himself end-played,' he declared. 'It shouldn't be beyond a self-proclaimed expert to keep the right cards!'

9.   The Last Minute Substitute

The Cahalan Cup was the premier knock-out competition in Hampshire and qualified for the award of national green points. Even though the Abbot had been a Grandmaster for more than ten years, he still regarded green points as one of the world's most precious commodities. He was happy indeed that the monastery's first-round opponents were an unknown team from the north of the county. He was less entranced to hear that Brother Xavier had woken up on the morning of the match suffering from a heavy bout of influenza.

'Goodness me!' exclaimed the Abbot. 'Did Xavier forget we had a Cahalan Cup match tonight?'

'Did he have any choice in the matter?' queried Brother Lucius. 'Anyway, we can hardly postpone the match at this late stage. I suppose we'll have to concede.'

Claude Yorke-Smith, the Abbot's brother who was visiting the monastery, stepped forward. 'No problem, is there?' he declared. 'I can partner Hugo.'

The Abbot had rarely heard a more senseless proposition. Claude was not even a member of the Hampshire Bridge Association.

'Good thinking,' Brother Lucius replied. 'We'll have to find you a cassock and remember to refer to you as Brother Xavier during the match. No reason why that shouldn't work.'

Any qualms the Abbot might have had were swiftly brushed aside. Half a green point for beating a bunch of social players who had probably never experienced the second round of the event? It was an opportunity not to be missed.

The Abbot liked to arrive somewhat late for matches, aiming to unsettle the opponents. On this occasion the traffic was lighter than usual and his ancient Morris Minor pulled up outside a large thatched cottage at the appointed hour of 7pm.

The match was soon underway. From the Abbot's point of view, the room was uncomfortably hot. That was the downside of away matches against elderly opponents. The central heating was always turned to the maximum level. Wearing normal clothes it would be easy enough to remove a pullover or jacket. If he were to remove his cassock, the ladies present would doubtless recoil in horror.

This was an early board:

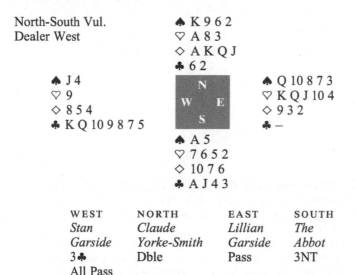

North-South Vul.
Dealer West

North hand: ♠ K 9 6 2 ♡ A 8 3 ◇ A K Q J ♣ 6 2

West hand: ♠ J 4 ♡ 9 ◇ 8 5 4 ♣ K Q 10 9 8 7 5

East hand: ♠ Q 10 8 7 3 ♡ K Q J 10 4 ◇ 9 3 2 ♣ —

South hand: ♠ A 5 ♡ 7 6 5 2 ◇ 10 7 6 ♣ A J 4 3

WEST	NORTH	EAST	SOUTH
Stan	*Claude*	*Lillian*	*The*
Garside	*Yorke-Smith*	*Garside*	*Abbot*
3♣	Dble	Pass	3NT
All Pass			

Stan Garside, who had spent most of the afternoon tending his allotment, led the ♣K against 3NT. The ♣2 was played from dummy, East discarding the ♠3, and the Abbot decided to duck the trick. Noting his partner's choice of discard, West switched to the ♡9 at Trick 2. The Abbot played low in dummy and Lillian Garside overtook with the ♡10. When she continued with the ♡K, West discarded the ♣10 and the Abbot won in the dummy.

The Abbot was well pleased with his progress so far. West would soon be left with nothing but clubs in his hand. Let's see how he enjoyed proceedings then!

The Abbot played four rounds of diamonds, throwing a heart, and continued with the ace and king of spades. West had played all six of his cards outside the club suit and was now ripe for an end-play. This position remained:

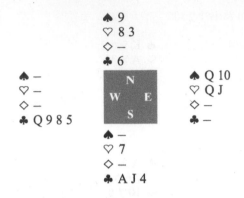

```
                    ♠ 9
                    ♡ 8 3
                    ◇ —
                    ♣ 6
      ♠ —                        ♠ Q 10
      ♡ —           N            ♡ Q J
      ◇ —        W     E         ◇ —
      ♣ Q 9 8 5     S            ♣ —
                    ♠ —
                    ♡ 7
                    ◇ —
                    ♣ A J 4
```

'Club, please,' instructed the Abbot. He followed with the ♣4 from his hand and faced his remaining cards. 'You have to lead back into my ace-jack of clubs,' he informed the elderly West player. 'An elegant +600, even if I say so myself.'

Stan Garside surveyed the position. If he won the trick, the overbearing declarer was right. But, wait a moment, what would happen if he played the ♣5, allowing dummy's ♣6 to win? It was surely worth a try, rather than leading into declarer's club tenace.

When Stan Garside placed the ♣5 on the table, the Abbot stared at the card in disbelief. What on earth had happened?

Lillian Garside smiled brightly. 'I think I make the last three tricks,' she said. 'That's one down.'

Claude Yorke-Smith glared across the table. 'Play dummy's ♣6 at Trick 1!' he exclaimed. 'In the West Country, such a play would be automatic. How can West duck if dummy still has the ♣2?'

The Abbot winced. What was Claude thinking about, mentioning the West Country? Had he forgotten he was meant to be Brother Xavier? As for suggesting that anyone might consider playing dummy's ♣6 at Trick 1, it was hard to imagine a more fatuous observation.

'If you're not going to play 3NT properly, pass out my double,' Claude Yorke-Smith continued. 'We get two spades, one heart, three diamonds and a couple of trumps. Oh dear – that's 800!'

'Are you normally so harsh on your partner?' enquired Lillian Garside. 'I'm sure he's trying his best. I didn't expect such criticism from a man of the cloth.'

The Abbot had rarely heard such wise words. 'It's a cross I have to bear,' he observed piously.

At the other table, Brother Lucius and Brother Paulo faced two stalwart churchgoers, Lucy and Bill Kingley.

Neither Vul.
Dealer South

```
                    ♠ 8 5 4
                    ♡ 10 4
                    ◇ 10 5 2
                    ♣ A Q 8 6 2
    ♠ 10 7 3              N              ♠ J 9 6 2
    ♡ K Q 9 2                            ♡ –
    ◇ A Q 8 4      W         E           ◇ J 7 6 3
    ♣ 7 3                S               ♣ K J 10 9 4
                    ♠ A K Q
                    ♡ A J 8 7 6 5 3
                    ◇ K 9
                    ♣ 5
```

WEST	NORTH	EAST	SOUTH
Brother	*Lucy*	*Brother*	*Bill*
Paulo	*Kingley*	*Lucius*	*Kingley*
–	–	–	1♡
Pass	1NT	Pass	4♡
Dble	All Pass		

Brother Paulo's penalty double was no certainty, but it was his experience that lesser players tended to lose a trick in the play when they were doubled. Anyway, the trumps were breaking badly. Was there any law against partner having a useful card or two?

Brother Paulo led the ♣7 and down went the dummy. 'Only a minimum 6 points, I'm afraid,' observed Lucy Kingley. 'Sorry if you wanted more.'

'Play the ace,' said Bill Kingley. After the penalty double, it seemed that West would hold three or four trumps to the king-queen and almost certainly the ◇A. How could he avoid losing four red-suit tricks? Perhaps he could do one of those end-play throw-ins? That would be good in such an important match.

The ruddy-faced declarer ruffed a club in his hand, removing West's last card in the suit, and cashed his three top spades. West followed all the way, he was pleased to see, and his next move was to lead a low trump towards dummy. Paulo stepped in with the ♡Q and surveyed this end position:

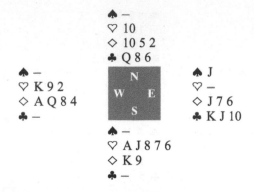

Brother Paulo, sitting West, considered his next move carefully. If he exited with a low trump, declarer would overtake dummy's ten with the jack, cash the ace of trumps and throw him back on lead with a fourth round of trumps. The same would happen if he exited with the king of trumps; he would be thrown in with the nine on the third round. In both cases, ace and another diamond would then allow declarer to score the ◇K. Was there any way to escape the end-play?

It seemed to Brother Paulo that he needed his partner to hold the ◇J. His mind made up, he exited with the ◇Q. Declarer won with the king and played a low trump towards the bare ten. Paulo rose with the king and led the ◇8 to East's jack. A return of the ♠J then promoted the ♡9 into the setting trick.

Paulo chuckled to himself. 'Not the soundest of penalty doubles, partner,' he said. 'Sorry about that. We were lucky to beat it, as it turned out.'

Back at the other table, the Abbot was somewhat puzzled at the lack of a good board on his card. The opponents were modest performers, it went without saying, but they had an uncanny knack of staying on their feet.

The players drew their cards for this deal:

Both Vul.
Dealer South

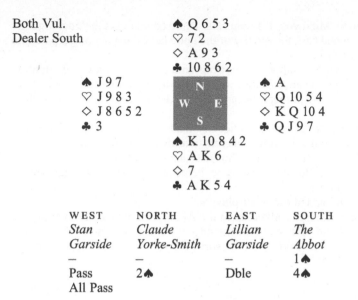

```
                    ♠ Q 6 5 3
                    ♡ 7 2
                    ◇ A 9 3
                    ♣ 10 8 6 2
  ♠ J 9 7                          ♠ A
  ♡ J 9 8 3          N             ♡ Q 10 5 4
  ◇ J 8 6 5 2     W     E          ◇ K Q 10 4
  ♣ 3                S             ♣ Q J 9 7
                    ♠ K 10 8 4 2
                    ♡ A K 6
                    ◇ 7
                    ♣ A K 5 4
```

WEST	NORTH	EAST	SOUTH
Stan	*Claude*	*Lillian*	*The*
Garside	*Yorke-Smith*	*Garside*	*Abbot*
–	–	–	1♠
Pass	2♠	Dble	4♠
All Pass			

Stan Garside lost no time in leading his singleton ♣3. With the air of someone doing something extremely clever, his wife contributed the ♣7 to the trick.

The Abbot won with the ace and saw that the game was his unless he lost two tricks in each black suit. Expecting East to hold the ♠A to make up the points for her double, he crossed to the ◇A and called for a low spade. When Lillian Garside won with the ♠A and returned the ♣Q, the Abbot looked up to make sure that he had the other players' full attention. He then followed with the ♣4 from his hand. West discarded a diamond and East continued with the ♣9. The Abbot played the ♣5 and the contract was then guaranteed. West was welcome to score a ruff because he was ruffing a loser. The Abbot ruffed the diamond return, drew trumps and claimed the balance.

'Dull hands so far,' exclaimed Claude Yorke-Smith.

The Abbot stared at his brother in disbelief. Dull hands? Had he not followed the play of that last hand at all?

'That's true,' said Stan Garside. 'Apart from that 3NT near the beginning, the rest of the boards look pretty flat.'

The first half drew to a close and the monastery team found themselves only 9 IMPs in the lead. The Abbot's disappointment was somewhat mollified by the appearance of the half-time refreshments. He had rarely seen tastier-looking scones! Clotted cream too, and what looked like home-made raspberry jam. It took him back to his childhood. Mind you, if Lucius and Paulo couldn't get their act together in the second half, the quality of the good ladies' baking might pale into insignificance.

Lucy Kingley tapped her teacup with a spoon to draw the attention of the other players. 'Before we enjoy Lillian's wonderful scones,' she said, 'it would perhaps be appropriate for the Abbot to say a short grace.'

The Abbot put down his heavily loaded plate and stepped forward. 'May we, and all bridge players worldwide, show compassion and understanding to partners who occasionally fall from perfection,' he declared. 'To do otherwise is to demean the great game that we all enjoy and love.'

'Amen,' added the other players.

Lillian Garside walked up to the Abbot, who was about to enjoy the first mouthful of a scone plastered with cream and jam. 'Those were fine words,' she said. 'I felt so sorry for you when you messed up that 3NT contract.'

10.   Brother Xavier's Reputation

The three monks had been careful to refer to Claude Yorke-Smith as Brother Xavier throughout the match and the subterfuge had proved successful so far. The monastery team led by a modest 9 IMPs at the interval and this was an early board in the second half:

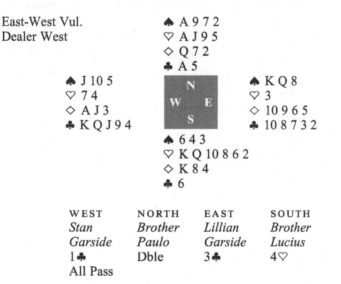

East-West Vul.
Dealer West

♠ A 9 7 2
♡ A J 9 5
◇ Q 7 2
♣ A 5

♠ J 10 5
♡ 7 4
◇ A J 3
♣ K Q J 9 4

♠ K Q 8
♡ 3
◇ 10 9 6 5
♣ 10 8 7 3 2

♠ 6 4 3
♡ K Q 10 8 6 2
◇ K 8 4
♣ 6

WEST	NORTH	EAST	SOUTH
Stan	*Brother*	*Lillian*	*Brother*
Garside	*Paulo*	*Garside*	*Lucius*
1♣	Dble	3♣	4♡
All Pass			

West led the ♣K and Brother Paulo laid out his eminently respectable dummy. Brother Lucius inspected it thoughtfully, noting that there were two potential losers in both spades and diamonds. One of the diamond losers could be avoided if West held ◇A-x or if the spades split 3-3 and provided a discard. Mind you, the discard might have to be established without allowing East to win the lead twice in spades. Otherwise he might make two damaging diamond leads from his side of the table.

Lucius saw that he could set up the spades safely if West held three cards including the king. He would lead towards the ♠A, ducking if the ♠K appeared. Otherwise he would put up the ♠A and West would then have to win one of the ducked rounds of spades.

Lucius was about to point at dummy's ♣A when a better way of playing the contract flashed into his mind. How had he missed it? Of course, he should duck the first round of clubs! Then the contract would make on any 3-3 spade break. 'Play low,' he said.

When Stan Garside continued with a second round of clubs, Lucius won with dummy's ace and discarded a spade from his hand. After drawing trumps in two rounds, he played ace and another spade. East won and switched to the ◇10, which was run to dummy's queen. Brother Lucius then ruffed a third round of spades. The suit divided 3-3 and he was able to claim the contract, discarding a diamond loser on the long spade.

Lucius smiled wryly. 'Your partner's getting a bit old, Paulo,' he declared. 'I nearly missed the winning line!'

At the other table the Abbot and his brother faced the Kingleys. 'Are you two related in any way?' enquired Lucy Kingley. 'You have a strong facial resemblance.'

'No, no,' replied the Abbot. 'Brother Xavier hails from the West Country. I've always lived in Hampshire.'

'It's amusing that you refer to him as a Brother,' observed Lucy Kingley. 'That rather backs up my point!'

The Abbot summoned a polite smile. Goodness me, Claude was one of the plainest-looking men ever born. How on earth had this woman managed to spot a similarity?

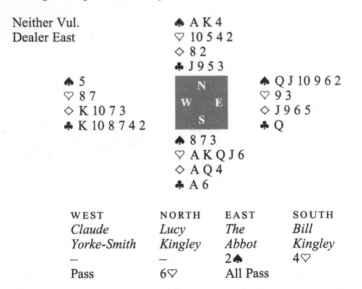

Neither Vul.
Dealer East

```
                        ♠ A K 4
                        ♡ 10 5 4 2
                        ◇ 8 2
                        ♣ J 9 5 3
    ♠ 5                                  ♠ Q J 10 9 6 2
    ♡ 8 7                                ♡ 9 3
    ◇ K 10 7 3                           ◇ J 9 6 5
    ♣ K 10 8 7 4 2                       ♣ Q
                        ♠ 8 7 3
                        ♡ A K Q J 6
                        ◇ A Q 4
                        ♣ A 6
```

WEST	NORTH	EAST	SOUTH
Claude	*Lucy*	*The*	*Bill*
Yorke-Smith	*Kingley*	*Abbot*	*Kingley*
–	–	2♠	4♡
Pass	6♡	All Pass	

Claude Yorke-Smith led his singleton spade and Lucy Kingley laid out her dummy. 'If you're worth ten tricks, Bill, my top spades should be enough for twelve.'

'Very nice hand, my dear,' Bill Kingley replied. Whether the slam could be made was another matter but it didn't cost anything to be pleasant.

'If you can ruff a diamond as well, it might come to thirteen,' his wife continued. 'Still, I didn't want to be too ambitious.'

The Abbot closed his eyes for a brief moment. Was the woman ever going to keep quiet? If she fancied herself as a commentator on the game, she should display her talents on *Bridge Base Online*. Meanwhile, there was no need to destroy everyone's concentration during a green-point match.

Bill Kingley won the spade lead in dummy and drew trumps in two rounds. When he played the ♣A, he was interested to see the queen fall from the Abbot. That gave him a chance! If he could set up a trick with dummy's ♣J, he could discard the spade loser and would then only need a successful diamond finesse.

When a second round of clubs was led, Claude Yorke-Smith rose with the king and the Abbot discarded a spade. These cards remained:

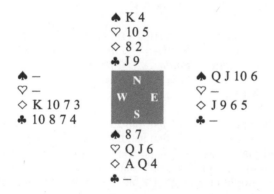

```
                    ♠ K 4
                    ♡ 10 5
                    ◇ 8 2
                    ♣ J 9
      ♠ —                         ♠ Q J 10 6
      ♡ —                         ♡ —
      ◇ K 10 7 3                  ◇ J 9 6 5
      ♣ 10 8 7 4                  ♣ —
                    ♠ 8 7
                    ♡ Q J 6
                    ◇ A Q 4
                    ♣ —
```

Claude Yorke-Smith did not like the look of the situation. Should he have refused to play the ♣K? A club return at this stage was no good; it would allow declarer to finesse dummy's nine. Like it or not, he would have to switch to a diamond. Bill Kingley won West's diamond switch with the queen and claimed the remaining tricks. 'I can ruff a diamond and discard the spade loser on the ♣J.'

The Abbot looked across the table. 'What happens if you duck the second club?' he enquired.

'It's no good,' Claude Yorke-Smith replied. 'He wins, ruffs a club, crosses to the other top spade and leads the last club, discarding a spade. I'm end-played, just the same.'

Bill Kingley turned to his left. 'Perhaps you should exit with a club instead of a diamond?' he suggested. 'I can finesse the ♣9 and take two discards but I think that leaves me a trick short.'

The Abbot gritted his teeth. Had the valuable notion of counting declarer's tricks not reached the West Country yet?

Meanwhile, at the other table, they were playing this deal:

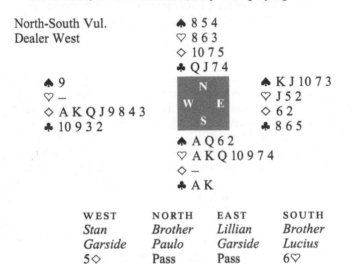

North-South Vul.
Dealer West

♠ 8 5 4
♡ 8 6 3
♢ 10 7 5
♣ Q J 7 4

♠ 9
♡ —
♢ A K Q J 9 8 4 3
♣ 10 9 3 2

♠ K J 10 7 3
♡ J 5 2
♢ 6 2
♣ 8 6 5

♠ A Q 6 2
♡ A K Q 10 9 7 4
♢ —
♣ A K

WEST	NORTH	EAST	SOUTH
Stan	*Brother*	*Lillian*	*Brother*
Garside	*Paulo*	*Garside*	*Lucius*
5♢	Pass	Pass	6♡
All Pass			

When the opening bid of 5♢ ran to him, Brother Lucius spent a moment or two gazing at his fine hand. It would be rather ambitious to bid a grand slam, hoping that partner could cover his spade losers. Surely the odds favoured a small slam, though. Even just the ♠J in Paulo's hand might be enough. He bid 6♡, ending the auction, and the ♢A was led.

'I fear that my hand is as bad as yours is good,' announced Brother Paulo, as he laid out the dummy.

'Could be worse,' replied Brother Lucius. There was nothing useful in spades, it was true. If trumps split 2-1, however, he could reach dummy with a trump to enjoy the two blocked club winners.

Brother Lucius ruffed with the ♡9 and played the ace of trumps, not particularly surprised when West discarded a diamond. Fortunately, dummy's remaining trumps were good enough to force an entry. He unblocked the two top clubs from his hand and continued with the ♡7, overtaken with dummy's ♡8. Lillian Garside won with the trump jack and returned a diamond. Lucius ruffed with the ♡10 and reached dummy by playing the ♡4 to dummy's ♡6. He discarded two spades on the ♣Q-J and took a successful spade finesse for the contract.

'I'm not sure Bill and Lucy will make that one,' observed Stan Garside. 'Perhaps I should have sacrificed in Seven Diamonds. If I lose three clubs and a spade, that's only 800.'

Brother Paulo leaned forward. 'On a trump lead, you would have to lose four clubs,' he said. 'I can play another trump when I win the third round of clubs.'

Back at the other table they had reached the final board:

```
Neither Vul.              ♠ A K J 8
Dealer North              ♡ J 10 5
                          ◇ Q
                          ♣ A Q 8 4 2
      ♠ 9 3                   N              ♠ 10 7 5 2
      ♡ K 9 2                                ♡ A
      ◇ 10 8 5 4 3 2      W       E          ◇ A 7 6
      ♣ 9 6                   S              ♣ K J 10 7 3
                          ♠ Q 6 4
                          ♡ Q 8 7 6 4 3
                          ◇ K J 9
                          ♣ 5
```

WEST	NORTH	EAST	SOUTH
Claude	*Lucy*	*The*	*Bill*
Yorke-Smith	*Kingley*	*Abbot*	*Kingley*
–	1♣	Pass	1♡
Pass	1♠	Pass	2♡
Pass	4♡	All Pass	

The ♠9 was led and North laid out her dummy. 'Would you like me to go just Three Hearts on this, Bill?' she asked.

'No, that's fine,' her husband replied. Now, how could he give the contract his best shot? There seemed to be only three losers – two trumps and the ◇A. Still, maybe the opponents could manage a spade ruff too. What could he do to prevent that?

Bill Kingley won the spade lead with dummy's jack and called for the ◇Q. The Abbot rose with the ace and returned a second round of spades. Declarer won with the queen and proceeded to discard dummy's ♠A and ♠K on his two diamond winners. With the risk of a spade ruff averted, he led a trump to the jack and East's ace. When the Abbot returned the ♠10, West discarded a club and dummy ruffed with the ♡5. These cards remained:

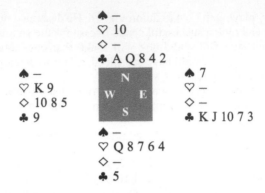

```
              ♠ —
              ♡ 10
              ◇ —
              ♣ A Q 8 4 2
♠ —                              ♠ 7
♡ K 9          N                 ♡ —
◇ 10 8 5    W     E              ◇ —
♣ 9            S                 ♣ K J 10 7 3
              ♠ —
              ♡ Q 8 7 6 4
              ◇ —
              ♣ 5
```

Bill Kingley smiled reassuringly at his wife. 'Ten of trumps, please,' he said. East showed out and Claude Yorke-Smith won with the king. Declarer won the club return with dummy's ace and returned to his hand with a club ruff. That was his intention, anyway, but West overruffed with the ♡9 and that was one down.

Claude Yorke-Smith peered over his glasses at the declarer. 'Oh dear, oh dear,' he exclaimed. 'You needed to cash the ♣A before playing the second trump. I can't lock you in dummy then.'

The Abbot's mouth fell open. That was pretty rude, even by Claude's lamentable standards. It had been a good effort by the elderly declarer, avoiding the spade ruff. Only the unlucky club break had defeated him.

Lucy Kingley had rarely encountered such poor manners. 'I hope you don't mind me saying this, Brother Xavier,' she declared, 'but your constant criticism of other players is spoiling everyone's enjoyment. Were you not listening when the Abbot spoke so wisely during his grace?

'I'm sure Brother Xavier will heed your advice in future,' said the Abbot, rising to his feet with a saintly air. 'The others have finished, I think. Time to compare scores!'

The Abbot was relieved to find that the monastery team had won by a healthy 27 IMPs. More importantly, their last-minute illegal substitution had escaped detection. Whether it had been worth the risk, it was too early to say. It would depend on how many green points they picked up in the remainder of the event.

11.   The Abbot's Careless Defence

Claude Yorke-Smith's visit had not gone particularly well and the Abbot was relieved when the day arrived for him to return to his home in Devon.

'There's a fast train at 10.40,' said the Abbot. 'I assume you would like me to give you a lift to the station?'

'Didn't I tell you?' Claude Yorke-Smith replied. 'Mavis called me on my mobile last night. Since we don't have any guests booked at the hotel, she suggested that I stay on for another few days.'

For a moment the Abbot closed his eyes. 'I see,' he replied. 'Do I take it you'll be playing in the pairs tonight?'

'Might as well, I suppose,' his brother replied. 'Mind you, I wasn't too impressed with our score a week ago. I'll be making a few changes to our convention card.'

'If you think I'm going to sign up to such atrocities as Ghestem and weak jump overcalls, you're mistaken,' said the Abbot firmly. 'My methods have served me well over the years.'

Claude Yorke-Smith laughed at this. 'Times have moved on, Hugo!'

The evening pairs session was into its fourth round when the novices, Brother Cameron and Brother Damien, arrived at the Abbot's table.

'You still with us?' queried Brother Cameron, as he slumped into the South seat.

The Abbot's eyes bulged. 'How dare you address a valued guest in that tone?' he demanded. 'Your manners are a disgrace to the monastery.'

'Sorry,' said Brother Cameron. 'Didn't mean to be rude. I just thought that Mr Yorke-Smith was going back today.'

'I have invited him to stay for a few extra days,' continued the Abbot. He pointed a finger at the board awaiting them. 'It's you to speak first on this one.'

North-South Vul.
Dealer South

<pre>
                    ♠ K Q J 8 5
                    ♡ 7 4
                    ♢ J 7 5 3
                    ♣ J 6
    ♠ 3 2   ♠ 6
    ♡ A 9 8 3 2   N   ♡ Q J 10 6
    ♢ 8 2   W   E   ♢ K 10 9
    ♣ K Q 10 4   S   ♣ 9 7 5 3 2
                    ♠ A 10 9 7 4
                    ♡ K 5
                    ♢ A Q 6 4
                    ♣ A 8
</pre>

WEST	NORTH	EAST	SOUTH
The	*Brother*	*Claude*	*Brother*
Abbot	*Damien*	*Yorke-Smith*	*Cameron*
—	—	—	1♠
Pass	4♠	All Pass	

The Abbot led the ♣K and inspected the dummy disapprovingly. Pre-empting with five-card support was all very well, but surely Three Spades was enough on that hand, vulnerable against not.

Brother Cameron won the club lead with the ace and drew trumps with the ace and king. A finesse of the ♢Q proved successful and he continued with the ♢A. Both defenders followed but the king refused to drop. Brother Cameron paused to assess the situation. If he played another round of diamonds, East would win and put the contract at risk with a heart switch. Fortunately there was a remedy available.

Brother Cameron exited with a club and the Abbot had to win the trick in the West seat. Claude Yorke-Smith had shown an odd number of clubs, following with the two and the three. Since declarer held five spades to East's one, the Abbot was fairly certain that East held five clubs rather than three. Unwilling to give a ruff-and-discard by playing a third round of clubs, he exited with ace and another heart.

Brother Cameron won with the ♡K and faced his remaining cards by way of a claim. 'You make a diamond trick,' he said.

'Nothing I could do,' the Abbot explained to his partner. 'If I play a club instead, that gives a ruff-and-discard.'

'Obviously,' Claude Yorke-Smith replied. 'You could have done something in the bidding, of course. What's wrong with a Two Heart overcall? Five Hearts our way is only a 300 touch.'

'A two-level overcall on five to the ace?' protested the Abbot.

'Passing on a shapely collection like that might have been good enough thirty years ago,' Claude Yorke-Smith continued. 'The players at our club wouldn't dream of passing.'

On the next round the Abbot faced Brother Richard and Brother Hubert.

East-West Vul.
Dealer South

	♠ A 10 8	
	♡ 7 5	
	◇ K 2	
	♣ A 10 8 6 5 2	

♠ Q 5 4 2		♠ 3
♡ J 6	N	♡ Q 10 9 4 2
◇ Q J 10 9 8 5	W E	◇ 6 3
♣ Q	S	♣ K J 9 7 3

	♠ K J 9 7 6	
	♡ A K 8 3	
	◇ A 7 4	
	♣ 4	

WEST	NORTH	EAST	SOUTH
Claude	*Brother*	*The*	*Brother*
Yorke-Smith	Hubert	*Abbot*	*Richard*
–	–	–	1♠
3◇	4♠	Pass	4NT
Pass	5♡	Pass	6♠
All Pass			

Claude Yorke-Smith led the ◇Q and down went the dummy. The Abbot eyed the ◇K with a resigned air. Claude had ventured a weak jump overcall on a queen-high suit, vulnerable against not. How much would that have cost if they'd been doubled?

Brother Richard liked the look of the cards his partner had laid out. There were five side-suit winners. If he could add seven trump tricks, the slam would be his. 'Play the king,' he said.

Brother Richard continued with the ♣A and the two top hearts in his hand. When he led a third round of hearts, West discarded a diamond and he ruffed with the ♠8. East followed when a diamond was led to the ace and declarer ruffed his last heart with the ♠10. These cards remained:

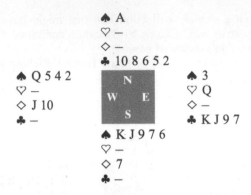

```
                    ♠ A
                    ♡ —
                    ◇ —
                    ♣ 10 8 6 5 2
    ♠ Q 5 4 2                        ♠ 3
    ♡ —            N                  ♡ Q
    ◇ J 10      W     E               ◇ —
    ♣ —            S                  ♣ K J 9 7
                    ♠ K J 9 7 6
                    ♡ —
                    ◇ 7
                    ♣ —
```

'Club, please,' said Brother Richard.

He ruffed the club with the ♠K and continued by ruffing his last diamond with the ♠A. He then faced his remaining trumps, conceding just one trick to the trump queen.

'Nicely played, partner,' said Brother Hubert.

'Not too difficult,' Brother Richard replied. 'I was always going to make it once a trump wasn't led.'

Brother Hubert perked up in his seat. A trump lead would have beaten it? Excellent! He could add the deal to his impending bestseller on trump leads. He turned towards Claude Yorke-Smith. 'Did you not consider a trump lead?' he asked. 'It's usually best against a slam.'

Aggravated as the Abbot was, after a near-certain bottom, this was a moment to be savoured. How many times had he suffered Brother Hubert's absurd pronouncements on trump leads? It was only fair that Claude should feel the burden on this occasion.

The Abbot nodded wisely. 'A trump lead and declarer has no chance. Do you see, Claude? He can only ruff two of his three red-suit losers and he still has to lose a trick to the trump queen.'

'Preposterous suggestion!' Yorke-Smith exclaimed. 'Of course I'm not leading from the queen of trumps.'

'I'll send you a copy of my book, once I manage to get it published,' Brother Hubert continued. 'I devoted a whole chapter to deals where you have to lead a trump, despite an awkward honour holding in the suit.'

A few rounds later, the Abbot and his brother faced the monastery's weakest pair.

'I could hardly have been more unlucky on the last board,' Brother Aelred observed, as he took his seat. 'I nearly always draw trumps straight away. I decided not to and . . . would you believe it? The opening lead was a singleton and his partner gave him a ruff! If I'd drawn trumps, I would have made it.'

The Abbot sighed deeply. No doubt this preposterous lapse of concentration had been against one of the monastery's stronger pairs, who would finish ahead of him as a result. Was it too much to hope that Brother Aelred would continue to distribute good scores on the present round?

Hoping for the best, the Abbot drew his cards for this deal:

```
Both Vul.                    ♠ K 4
Dealer South                 ♡ A 7 2
                             ◇ 7 6 3 2
                             ♣ 10 8 4 3
        ♠ —                               ♠ 10 9 8 7 3
        ♡ J 10 9 8 4      N               ♡ K Q 6 5
        ◇ J 10 8 5     W     E            ◇ Q 4
        ♣ J 9 7 5         S               ♣ K Q
                             ♠ A Q J 6 5 2
                             ♡ 3
                             ◇ A K 9
                             ♣ A 6 2
```

WEST	NORTH	EAST	SOUTH
Brother	*Claude*	*Brother*	*The*
Aelred	*Yorke-Smith*	*Michael*	*Abbot*
–	–	–	1♠
Pass	1NT	Pass	3♠
Pass	4♠	All Pass	

The ♡J was led and the Abbot surveyed the dummy in disbelief. There were ten tricks on top in both spades and no-trumps. +630 would be a top and +620 would be a bottom. What was Claude thinking of? Surely it was obvious that his ♠K would solidify the suit? He held the ♡A and his four-card length in each of the minors surely meant that the defenders could run no great number of tricks there. If only the North and South cards had been switched! He would have bid the obvious 3NT and their scorecard would have benefited accordingly. 'Ace, please,' said the Abbot.

The Abbot was about to draw trumps when a thought occurred to him. What if the trumps were 5-0? He would then have only five trump tricks and four side-suit winners. It seemed that he should perhaps aim for two heart ruffs in his hand, to assure six trump tricks. Not that it was likely to make any difference, of course.

The Abbot ruffed a heart in his hand and led a trump towards dummy. A look of ecstasy came to his face as West discarded a heart. After winning with the ♠K, he ruffed another heart in his hand. He had four tricks before him. Three further trump winners and three top cards in the minors brought the total to ten.

'That could be a top for us,' said Brother Michael. 'I had five good trumps and 12 points! Most players would have doubled.'

Claude Yorke-Smith inspected the score-sheet. 'Very poor standard,' he observed. 'Three pairs went down in Four Spades and two went down in 3NT. At my club in Devon the plus column would be full to bursting point!'

The Abbot's next opponents were Lucius and Paulo.

Brother Lucius chuckled as he took his seat. 'Next week you'll have to play with the real Brother Xavier!' he observed.

The Abbot winced at this reference to the Cahalan Cup match where, contrary all the regulations, Claude had replaced the flu-stricken Brother Xavier. 'Keep your voice down,' he said. 'Most of our brethren are unaware of the situation. If the authorities find out about it, I hate to think of the consequences.'

This was the first board of the round:

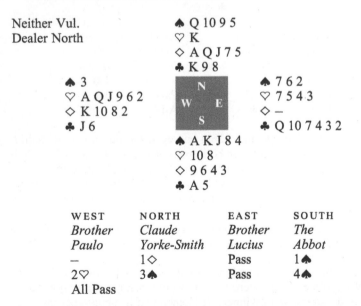

Neither Vul.
Dealer North

♠ Q 10 9 5
♡ K
◇ A Q J 7 5
♣ K 9 8

♠ 3
♡ A Q J 9 6 2
◇ K 10 8 2
♣ J 6

♠ 7 6 2
♡ 7 5 4 3
◇ —
♣ Q 10 7 4 3 2

♠ A K J 8 4
♡ 10 8
◇ 9 6 4 3
♣ A 5

WEST	NORTH	EAST	SOUTH
Brother	*Claude*	*Brother*	*The*
Paulo	*Yorke-Smith*	*Lucius*	*Abbot*
–	1◇	Pass	1♠
2♡	3♠	Pass	4♠
All Pass			

Brother Paulo led the ◇2 against the Abbot's spade game and down went the dummy. Goodness me, thought the Abbot, they were close to a slam on these values! Now, what was this diamond lead? With anyone but Paulo in the West seat, the odds of finding the ◇K onside would be poor. Expecting good diamonds in the dummy, Paulo would think nothing of leading a deceptive two from ◇K-2, aiming to deter declarer from finessing. If so, he had chosen the wrong declarer for his embarrassingly obvious tactics. 'Play the queen,' said the Abbot.

Brother Lucius ruffed in the East seat and returned the ♡7. Winning with the ace, Brother Paulo continued with the ◇10. The Abbot covered with dummy's ◇J, ruffed by East, and that was the first three tricks to the defenders. West's ◇K-8 was still worth a trick and the contract went one down.

'Strange one,' observed Brother Lucius. 'You need to play low from dummy on the first trick, Abbot. I still get two ruffs but the remaining ◇A-Q-J protects you from a fourth loser there.'

'Oh dear, you had the nine, did you?' exclaimed Claude Yorke-Smith. 'Yes, low from dummy works very well.'

'I assume you're both joking,' retorted the Abbot. 'Suppose I play low and Paulo has led from ◇K-8-2 or ◇K-2, knowing that the good diamonds lie over him. How foolish would I look then?'

Claude Yorke-Smith sat back in his chair, considering the matter. 'It's difficult to say,' he replied. 'Probably about the same.'

In the final round of the session the Abbot faced his regular partner, Brother Xavier, who was partnered by the black-bearded Brother Zac. No doubt fate had treated them kindly and they would finish ahead of him and Claude. Strange as it was, new partnerships often did well on their first outing. With a limited number of conventions available, there was less opportunity for bidding misunderstandings. Not, of course, that he had the slightest intention of asking Brother Xavier how well he had done.

'Sorry to have deprived you of the Abbot's company,' said Claude Yorke-Smith as Xavier took his seat. 'How have you done with your new partner?'

The Abbot beckoned for the first board to be put into position. What possible interest could there be in such small talk?

'Amazingly, we've done quite well,' Brother Xavier replied. 'No problems in the bidding, anyway.'

The Abbot tapped the table. 'Shall we play this one?' he said.

Brother Xavier was soon thumbing through his best hand of the evening:

North-South Vul.   ♠ 7 5 2
Dealer South   ♡ 3 2
                    ◇ A 10 7 4 2
                    ♣ J 3 2

```
      ♠ 3                    N            ♠ J 10 9 6
      ♡ Q 10 9 8 5      W       E        ♡ J 6 4
      ◇ 8 5                 S            ◇ Q J 6 3
      ♣ Q 9 8 7 4                        ♣ K 10
```

                    ♠ A K Q 8 4
                    ♡ A K 7
                    ◇ K 9
                    ♣ A 6 5

WEST	NORTH	EAST	SOUTH
Claude	*Brother*	*The*	*Brother*
Yorke-Smith	*Zac*	*Abbot*	*Xavier*
–	–	–	2♣
Pass	2◇	Pass	2♠
Pass	3♠	Pass	4♣
Pass	4◇	Pass	6♠
All Pass			

Claude Yorke-Smith led the ◇8 and down went the dummy. There was little to spare, Brother Xavier observed. He would need a 3-2 trump break, obviously, but there would still be a problem in avoiding two club losers. Perhaps his leap to 6♠ had been a bit precipitate. 'Small, please,' he said.

Brother Xavier won the Abbot's ◇J with the ◇K and played two top trumps, looking distinctly unimpressed when West showed out on the second round. With a certain trump trick against him, he would now need to dispose of both his club losers.

Deciding that he had to make something of dummy's diamond suit, Brother Xavier crossed to the ◇A. The ◇5 fell from West and he then called for the ◇10. The Abbot covered with the queen, ruffed by declarer, and Xavier then cashed the ♣A. Two top hearts and a heart ruff in dummy left these cards still to be played:

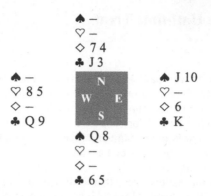

```
              ♠ —
              ♡ —
              ◇ 7 4
              ♣ J 3
   ♠ —                        ♠ J 10
   ♡ 8 5        N             ♡ —
   ◇ —       W     E          ◇ 6
   ♣ Q 9        S             ♣ K
              ♠ Q 8
              ♡ —
              ◇ —
              ♣ 6 5
```

'Play the ◇7,' said Brother Xavier, discarding a club from his hand. 'And the ◇4, please.'

The Abbot had no counter in the East seat. If he discarded the club king, declarer would ditch his last club loser and lose just one trick in trumps. When the Abbot eventually ruffed the last diamond, Brother Xavier threw his remaining club and claimed the last two tricks with the queen and eight of trumps.

The Abbot slumped back in his chair. It was nothing short of a miracle that the slam had succeeded. If Claude had chosen any opening lead except a diamond, declarer would have had no hope whatsoever.

'Not the best,' observed Claude Yorke-Smith.

'You can say that again,' retorted the Abbot. What in heaven's name had impelled Claude to lead a diamond?

'Surely it's obvious to play low on the diamond lead?' Yorke-Smith continued. 'He can't score four diamond tricks then.'

The Abbot blinked. Play low at Trick 1? Would that make any difference? Incredibly, it seemed that it would. Declarer would score three diamond tricks but not the four that he needed. He would have to lose a trump and a club.

'But what if your lead was a singleton?' the Abbot protested. 'That's much more likely than a doubleton. Playing low would surrender my trick in diamonds when I had a certain trump trick.'

Yorke-Smith shared a smile with Lucius and Paulo. 'Methinks he doth protest too much,' he declared. 'I may be exaggerating but back in Torquay I don't believe a single East player would have gone in with a diamond honour!'

12.   The Half-time Treat

'We'll soon be there,' said Bill Woodhead. 'The monastery doesn't provide any refreshments worthy of the name. Norma and I took the precaution of eating a full supper before we left.'

Pauline Quigley leaned forward from the Jaguar's back seat. 'Now you tell us!' she exclaimed. 'Stan and I haven't had a bite to eat. In the last round our opponents provided a wonderful spread and we were too full to take advantage of it.'

'Just margarine sandwiches, that's all you get at the monastery,' continued Bill Woodhead. 'They claim they have no money to spare. Judging from the size of Abbot Yorke-Smith, he doesn't restrict himself to margarine sandwiches the rest of the time.'

'The one to look out for is Brother Xavier,' said Norma Woodhead. 'He's a short man with glasses apparently. A golf friend of mine, Lucy Kingley, played them in the previous round and she found Brother Xavier very rude. He even criticized the way Lucy played a couple of hands and she's a very good player.'

The match was soon underway and the Abbot was happy to be back in partnership with Brother Xavier. This was an early board:

```
Both Vul.                ♠ 8 5 2
Dealer West              ♡ 9 8 6 5
                         ◇ 9 8 4 3
                         ♣ 7 3
         ♠ K Q 3                        ♠ 4
         ♡ A K J 4 2          N         ♡ 10 7 3
         ◇ K Q 10 7       W       E     ◇ J 6 5 2
         ♣ 2                  S         ♣ J 10 9 8 6
                         ♠ A J 10 9 7 6
                         ♡ Q
                         ◇ A
                         ♣ A K Q 5 4
```

WEST	NORTH	EAST	SOUTH
The	*Pauline*	*Brother*	*Stan*
Abbot	*Quigley*	*Xavier*	*Quigley*
1♡	Pass	Pass	2♡
Dble	Pass	Pass	4♠
Dble	All Pass		

The Abbot turned towards Mrs Quigley. Not expecting the monastery to be adequately heated, she was wearing an unusually thick home-made pullover. 'Your partner's 2♡?' he queried.

'Oh yes, sorry,' Mrs Quigley replied. 'It's not natural. I should have alerted it.'

The Abbot waited patiently for further information. Surely the fact that you were kitted out for a long mid-winter walk in Iceland did not excuse you from explaining partner's bidding?

'If he had a long string of hearts, he would probably have passed,' Mrs Quigley added.

For a brief moment the Abbot closed his eyes. 'Yes, but what did Two Hearts mean?'

'Well, we normally play Michaels,' came the reply, 'but when he rebids 4♠, it may be something different.'

The Abbot led the ♡K and down went the dummy. 'I do have three spades for you Stan,' Pauline Quigley observed. 'I didn't want to bid them when he doubled your Two Hearts in case you . . . well, in case you jumped to game in spades.'

Brother Xavier followed with the ♡3, showing an odd number of cards in the suit, and the ♡Q fell from declarer. The Abbot paused to consider his next move. If declarer had anything approaching a Michaels bid, his other suit was surely clubs. It seemed right to switch to the trump king at this stage. It would cost him a trump trick initially, no doubt. The trick might come back with interest if he was able to ruff a club subsequently and draw another round of trumps with the queen.

Stan Quigley, who kept himself in shape with a twice-weekly visit to the golf course, won the ♠K switch with the ace. With visions of a possible overtrick, he continued with the ♣A-K. The Abbot dashed these hopes by ruffing the second club honour with the ♠3. He was quick to lay down the ♠Q and this left declarer with an eventual club loser. The game was one down.

The Abbot sat back in his chair, an ecstatic gleam in his eye. What a defence! Suppose he'd continued woodenly with the ♡A at Trick 2 as Xavier would have done. Declarer would ruff and play the two top clubs. He could ruff with the ♠3 and switch to the ♠K, yes, but declarer would simply win and ruff his two club losers. The defenders would score just two trumps and a heart.

Brother Xavier turned towards the declarer. 'Interesting hand,' he said. 'I think you can do it if you play the ♣A and continue with a low club. I win the trick and have no trump to return.'

Pauline Quigley shared a glance with her husband. Was that the right thing to do, criticizing an opponent's play? Norma's friend had been quite right about Brother Xavier. Mind you, he wasn't particularly short and he wasn't wearing glasses. That was strange.

'To beat it for sure, Abbot, I think you have to lead the king of trumps at Trick 1,' continued Brother Xavier. 'That leaves you with a heart entry if declarer ducks a club subsequently.'

Pauline Quigley had heard enough. 'May I ask you something?' she said. 'Do you normally wear glasses?'

Before Brother Xavier could answer, he felt a sharp kick from across the table. What on earth was going on?

The Abbot had been quick to assess the situation. 'My partner is somewhat sensitive on the matter,' he declared. 'Sadly, he does have to wear glasses if the light is poor. This room is well lit, as you see.'

Pauline Quigley surveyed Brother Xavier disapprovingly. Sensitive to his own situation he might be, but not in the least considerate when it came to his feelings for others. It was hardly the attitude one would expect from a man of the cloth.

Meanwhile, Lucius and Paulo faced the Woodheads at the other table. The bidding was about to start on this board:

East-West Vul.
Dealer South

```
                    ♠ 2
                    ♡ K J 4 2
                    ◇ 10 8 7 6 2
                    ♣ 10 7 3
  ♠ A Q J 7 3          N           ♠ 9 8 5
  ♡ 8 6          W           E      ♡ 10 3
  ◇ K 5 4                           ◇ Q J 9 3
  ♣ Q J 5              S            ♣ K 8 6 4
                    ♠ K 10 6 4
                    ♡ A Q 9 7 5
                    ◇ A
                    ♣ A 9 2
```

WEST	NORTH	EAST	SOUTH
Bill	*Brother*	*Norma*	*Brother*
Woodhead	*Paulo*	*Woodhead*	*Lucius*
–	–	–	1♡
1♠	3♡	Pass	4♡
All Pass			

Bill Woodhead led the ♡8 and down went the dummy. 'Good gracious, you bid Three Hearts on that?' he queried.

'My partner's bid is pre-emptive after an overcall,' Brother Lucius explained. 'With another ace he would have bid Two Spades.'

Bill Woodhead scratched his head. What on earth would North have held for a raise to just Two Hearts? He certainly hadn't expected such wild bidding from a pair of monks.

Brother Lucius saw that the trump lead would almost certainly prevent him from ruffing three spades in dummy. West was unlikely to have led a singleton trump and he would surely persist with the suit when he won a spade trick. In that case it might be necessary to set up a diamond winner in dummy. How this could be done was another matter. He seemed to be one entry short, however the cards lay.

Brother Lucius cashed the ♢A and crossed to dummy with a trump, pleased to see the 2-2 break. After a diamond ruff in his hand, he continued with ace and another club. West won with the ♣J and continued with the ♣Q. Norma Woodhead overtook with the club ♣K and surveyed this end position from the East seat:

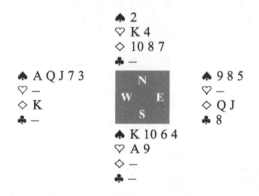

```
                    ♠ 2
                    ♡ K 4
                    ♢ 10 8 7
                    ♣ —
♠ A Q J 7 3                         ♠ 9 8 5
♡ —              N                  ♡ —
♢ K          W       E              ♢ Q J
♣ —              S                  ♣ 8
                    ♠ K 10 6 4
                    ♡ A 9
                    ♢ —
                    ♣ —
```

When the ♠9 appeared from East, Brother Lucius covered with the ♠10. Bill Woodhead won with the ♠J and had no good card to play. Since a spade would clearly allow declarer to score the ♠K as his tenth trick, he had to return the ♢K.

Brother Lucius ruffed in his hand and crossed to dummy with a spade ruff. He ruffed a further diamond in his hand and was then able to return to dummy with a second spade ruff to enjoy the established ♢10 as his tenth trick.

Brother Paulo chuckled to himself. 'I had just enough for you,' he observed. 'Give East my ♣10 and they could beat it.'

Norma Woodhead could never summon any interest in a deal once it had been played. She looked disapprovingly at Brother Paulo. It was typical of men to show off, displaying their knowledge of the game rather than getting on with the next board.

Brother Paulo turned towards Norma Woodhead. 'You see what would happen then?' he continued. 'When declarer plays the ♣A, your partner would unblock one of his honours! You gain the lead twice in clubs, with the ♣K and ♣10, and can rescue him from the end-play.'

'I certainly would have done,' declared Norma Woodhead, who had not followed a word of what Brother Paulo was saying. It was bad enough wasting time discussing the actual hand. Discussing a slightly different hand was intolerable.

Meanwhile, back at the other table, Stan Quigley had just arrived in a vulnerable game.

Both Vul.
Dealer North

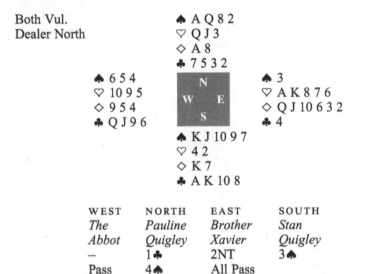

♠ A Q 8 2
♡ Q J 3
◇ A 8
♣ 7 5 3 2

♠ 6 5 4
♡ 10 9 5
◇ 9 5 4
♣ Q J 9 6

♠ 3
♡ A K 8 7 6
◇ Q J 10 6 3 2
♣ 4

♠ K J 10 9 7
♡ 4 2
◇ K 7
♣ A K 10 8

WEST	NORTH	EAST	SOUTH
The	*Pauline*	*Brother*	*Stan*
Abbot	*Quigley*	*Xavier*	*Quigley*
–	1♣	2NT	3♠
Pass	4♠	All Pass	

The Abbot led the ♡10, covered by the jack and king. When Brother Xavier switched to the ◇Q, declarer won with the ace and drew trumps in three rounds. All now depended on a helpful club break. Stan Quigley cashed the two top clubs and sat back in his chair when East discarded a diamond on the second round. That was unlucky! He cashed the ◇K, leaving these cards still out:

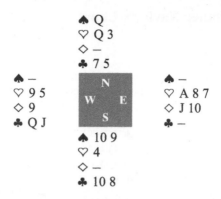

```
              ♠ Q
              ♡ Q 3
              ◇ —
              ♣ 7 5
♠ —                        ♠ —
♡ 9 5                      ♡ A 8 7
◇ 9                        ◇ J 10
♣ Q J                      ♣ —
              ♠ 10 9
              ♡ 4
              ◇ —
              ♣ 10 8
```

Stan Quigley led the ♡4, noting with interest the appearance of the lowly ♡5 on his left. 'Play the three, please, Pauline,' he said.

Brother Xavier won cheaply and played the ♡A, declarer throwing a club. On the diamond continuation Stan Quigley discarded his last club and ruffed in dummy. The game was made.

The Abbot's mouth dropped. What an incredibly lucky heart position for declarer! 'It's no good if I put in the ♡9,' he said. 'He covers with the queen and you have to win the third round.'

The half-time scoring was soon completed. 'Five IMPs to you?' queried Stan Quigley.

'Five, that's right,' the Abbot replied. 'Now, it was quite a long journey for you, I realize. I asked our chef, Brother Anthony, to prepare two extra-large platefuls of sandwiches.'

Bill Woodhead was not renowned for his tact. 'They wouldn't happen to be margarine sandwiches, would they?' he enquired.

'Monastery finances don't run to smoked salmon and Parma ham, I'm afraid,' replied the Abbot. 'If there's any money left over at the end of the month, we transfer it to our mission in Upper Bhumpopo. They've had a drought there for the last two years.'

'I quite like fish paste sandwiches, actually,' persisted Bill Woodhead. 'That wouldn't break the bank, would it? Or how about egg sandwiches? Don't you keep chickens here?'

Norma Woodhead winced at her husband's indiscretion. 'Bill has an unusual sense of humour, I'm afraid,' she informed the Abbot. ' I've always quite liked margarine.'

Brother Cameron and Brother Justine soon arrived, each carrying a heavily loaded plate of thick-cut sandwiches.

'One for you, Abbot?' asked a stony-faced Brother Cameron.

'Er . . . not at the moment,' the Abbot replied. 'Offer them to Mr and Mrs Woodhead here. Our guests must come first!'

13.   Brother Xavier's Lapse

At half-time in the second-round Hampshire Knockout match, the monastery led the Woodhead team by just 5 IMPs. Play resumed with the Abbot and Brother Xavier facing Mr and Mrs Woodhead.

```
Both Vul.                    ♠ 5 3
Dealer South                 ♡ Q 4 2
                             ◇ K J 10 6
                             ♣ J 8 4 2
        ♠ J 6                              ♠ 10 9 4
        ♡ J 10 9 7 5          N            ♡ 8 6 3
        ◇ 8 4 2          W         E       ◇ A Q 9
        ♣ 10 7 6              S            ♣ A K 9 5
                             ♠ A K Q 8 7 2
                             ♡ A K
                             ◇ 7 5 3
                             ♣ Q 3
```

WEST	NORTH	EAST	SOUTH
Bill	*Brother*	*Norma*	*The*
Woodhead	*Xavier*	*Woodhead*	*Abbot*
–	–	–	1♠
Pass	1NT	Pass	4♠
All Pass			

Bill Woodhead led the ♡J against the spade game and the Abbot won in his hand. He drew trumps, pleased to see the 3-2 break, and played the remaining heart honour in his hand. What now?

All would be well if he played a diamond to the jack and West held the queen. For that matter, he would make the contract if he guessed to rise with the ◇K and West held the ace. The lead would then be in dummy and he could discard one of his remaining diamonds on the ♡Q. Was anything better available?

The Abbot soon spotted an extra chance. Of course! He should play the ♣Q next. If East happened to hold the ace and king of clubs, she would be end-played. West would have led a club if he held the ace-king, so it was a one-in-three chance to find East with both club honours.

The Abbot led the ♣Q from his hand, East winning with the king. Norma Woodhead was on lead in this end position:

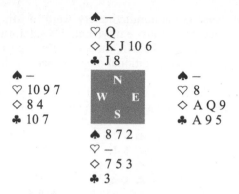

♠ —
♡ Q
◇ K J 10 6
♣ J 8

♠ —
♡ 10 9 7
◇ 8 4
♣ 10 7

♠ —
♡ 8
◇ A Q 9
♣ A 9 5

♠ 8 7 2
♡ —
◇ 7 5 3
♣ 3

East had no safe exit. Ace and another club would allow the Abbot to discard two diamonds from his hand, one on the ♣J and another on the ♡Q. A heart return instead would allow him to throw his last club, subsequently finessing against the diamond queen for an overtrick. A diamond return was equally hopeless.

Norma Woodhead eventually decided to return a heart and the Abbot soon had ten tricks pointing his way. He leaned to his right, viewing East's remaining cards with a look of ecstasy. She held all the missing high cards. On any other line of play he would have gone down!

'It's easier in 3NT, isn't it?' said Brother Xavier. 'I think I might have tried that on your hand.'

Norma Woodhead summoned her courage. It was time this Brother Xavier character learned how to behave at the bridge table. 'I hope you don't mind me mentioning this,' she said, 'but it would be a much more pleasant game if you didn't continually criticize the other players.'

The Abbot sucked in his right cheek. Marvellous! It was no more than Xavier deserved after failing to commend his world-class play on the deal.

'A friend of mine, Lucy Kingley, was in the team that you faced in the last round,' persisted Mrs Woodhead. 'She said exactly the same thing.'

Brother Xavier's mouth fell open. But . . . he hadn't even played in the previous round. He'd been struck down by 'flu and the Abbot's brother, Claude Yorke-Smith, had substituted for him. Had Claude pretended to be him, making his usual sarcastic comments in someone else's name? What unbelievable cheek!

'Your partner never makes any critical comments,' continued Mrs Woodhead. 'Neither do I or Bill. On this very hand a diamond lead, or even a club lead, would have beaten the game. I didn't say anything because I didn't want to hurt Bill's feelings.'

The Abbot, who had committed every word of Mrs Woodhead's speech to memory for future enjoyment, leaned forward. 'May I apologize on my partner's behalf,' he said. 'I'm sure there'll be no more infringements of the traditional etiquette that the three of us like to follow.'

At the other table, Lucius and Paulo had made a good start against Mr and Mrs Quigley. This was the fourth board of the set:

Neither Vul.
Dealer South

		♠ 9 7 4 3 2	
		♡ 5 4	
		◇ A Q 9 2	
		♣ K 4	
♠ J			♠ 8 5
♡ 10 9 7 3			♡ J 8 6 2
◇ 10 8 4			◇ K J 5
♣ Q J 10 8 3			♣ A 9 7 5
		♠ A K Q 10 6	
		♡ A K Q	
		◇ 7 6 3	
		♣ 6 2	

WEST	NORTH	EAST	SOUTH
Brother	*Pauline*	*Brother*	*Stan*
Paulo	*Quigley*	*Lucius*	*Quigley*
–	–	–	1♠
Pass	3♠	Pass	4♠
All Pass			

Brother Paulo led the ♣Q against the spade game. 'King, please,' said Stan Quigley, the moment dummy went down.

Brother Lucius won with the ace and returned the ♣5 to Paulo's ♣8. Declarer was none too pleased to see the ◇4 on the table next. 'Try the nine,' he said.

When Lucius won with the jack and exited safely with a heart, declarer was doomed. He won, drew trumps and conceded one down when a last-chance finesse of the ◇Q lost to the king.

Pauline Quigley looked uncertainly at her husband. 'Was that right, playing the ♣K at Trick 1?' she queried. 'If you play low, East has to win the second club and he can't play a diamond. I think you can catch him in an elimination ending then.'

Stan Quigley smiled at this suggestion. He turned towards Brother Paulo. 'Forgive my wife,' he said. 'I'm sure she didn't mean to insult your defence. If I let the ♣Q win, you'd have switched to a diamond, wouldn't you?'

'Yes, indeed,' replied Brother Paulo. He had no wish to cause marital disharmony but had declarer not noticed that he could then win with the ◇A, draw trumps and discard dummy's ♣K on the third round of hearts?

'You see, Pauline?' continued Stan Quigley. 'We're not playing against Muppets here.'

Back on the Abbot's table, they had reached the penultimate board of the match:

Both Vul.
Dealer South

```
                        ♠ A K Q 4
                        ♡ Q J 10
                        ◇ 9 6 4 2
                        ♣ 6 5
        ♠ 10 2            N            ♠ J 9 8 6 5
        ♡ 9 8 7 6 3   W       E        ♡ 5 4
        ◇ A Q            S            ◇ 8 7 5 3
        ♣ K J 8 7                      ♣ Q 3
                        ♠ 7 3
                        ♡ A K 2
                        ◇ K J 10
                        ♣ A 10 9 4 2
```

WEST	NORTH	EAST	SOUTH
Bill	*Brother*	*Norma*	*The*
Woodhead	*Xavier*	*Woodhead*	*Abbot*
–	–	–	1NT
Pass	2♣	Pass	2◇
Pass	3NT	All Pass	

Bill Woodhead led the ♡6 against 3NT and the Abbot paused briefly to make a plan. He had seven tricks on top and at least two more from the diamond suit. It was a pity in a way. If a clever play had been required to make the contract, there would have been a chance of gaining IMPs. On this lay-out, the Woodheads' pet poodle could land nine tricks. If they had a pet poodle.

The Abbot won the first trick in dummy and finessed the ◇J, losing to the queen. Sensing that declarer might have to rely on dummy's spades for entries later in the play, Bill Woodhead switched to the ♠10. The Abbot won in the dummy and played another diamond to the king and ace. A spade continuation removed dummy's last entry while the diamonds were blocked and the game went one down.

Brother Xavier thought back over the play. Had the Abbot not wasted dummy's heart entry? Suppose he won the first trick with the ♡A and crossed to a spade to take a diamond finesse. West would not be able to dislodge dummy's heart entry. Whether he returned a heart or a spade, the Abbot would be able to force out the ♢A and unblock his own last card in the suit. Dummy would still have a certain entry to the established ♢9.

'The spade switch was awkward for me,' declared the Abbot. 'No doubt Lucius and Paulo will find the same defence.'

Brother Xavier was itching to point out how the contract should have been made. After his earlier reprimand from Norma Woodhead, it seemed he would have to wait until the opponents had departed.

This was the last deal of the match:

East-West Vul.
Dealer East

	♠ J 5	
	♡ A K 5 3	
	♢ 7 5	
	♣ J 9 8 5 3	
♠ 10 9 7 3		♠ Q 8 6 4
♡ 9 6 4		♡ 2
♢ K J 8		♢ Q 10 6 4
♣ K 6 4		♣ Q 10 7 2
	♠ A K 2	
	♡ Q J 10 8 7	
	♢ A 9 3 2	
	♣ A	

WEST	NORTH	EAST	SOUTH
Bill	*Brother*	*Norma*	*The*
Woodhead	*Xavier*	*Woodhead*	*Abbot*
–	–	Pass	1♡
Pass	3♡	Pass	6♡
All Pass			

Bill Woodhead led the ♡4 and the Abbot sat back in his chair. This trump lead was a bit aggravating. After any other lead he could have scored three ruffs in the dummy. Perhaps something could be done with the club suit.

The Abbot won the trump lead in his hand and played the ♣A, no card of interest appearing. He cashed the two top spades and ruffed a spade in the dummy. Praying for one of the defenders to have started with ♣K-Q-x, he called for a club. Two more spot cards appeared and the Abbot slumped in his chair. He continued resignedly with ace and another diamond, but West won with the $\diamond$J and returned another trump. Only one diamond ruff could be taken and the slam was one down.

'Brother Hubert would pay good money for the deal,' declared the Abbot. 'The trump lead was the only one to beat me. Otherwise I can score three ruffs in the dummy.'

Norma Woodhead turned towards the Abbot. 'A trump lead is fairly normal against a slam, isn't it?' she said. 'You can hardly lead away from a side-suit honour when the opponents are likely to hold all the missing high cards.'

The monks reconvened to compare scores. The scores were neck and neck when they came to the last board, where the Abbot had gone down in 6$\heartsuit$. 'Minus 100,' he said.

'And plus 100,' announced Brother Lucius. 'Let's see . . . I make it we win by 3 IMPs.'

'Goodness me, that was a close one!' exclaimed the Abbot. 'You found the trump lead against Six Hearts on the last board?'

'Yes, but declarer never gave himself a real chance,' Lucius replied. 'A spade to the jack is best. East wins with the queen and has no trump to return. Declarer can discard a diamond on the third spade and take three diamond ruffs in dummy.'

'That's right,' said Brother Xavier.

'What do you mean that's right?' demanded the Abbot. 'You never mentioned it at the time.'

'And have them complaining to the committee about my ethics?' exclaimed Brother Xavier. 'What on earth happened when Claude stood in for me on the previous match?'

'Oh, nothing much, nothing at all,' replied the Abbot. 'Now, let's do our duty and offer our opponents a few words of consolation. Pull yourself together, Xavier. Surely you can summon a smile from somewhere?'

Part III Interlude at St Hilda's

14.   The Mother of Discipline's Verdict

It was three years since the Abbot had visited St Hilda's Convent. Sister Grace, a distant cousin of his, had been suffering from a mysterious illness and he felt it was his duty to lend support.

'Good to see you, Hugo,' said Sister Grace. 'I hope your drive here wasn't too onerous.'

'Well, I could certainly do with one of these modern cars that have air-conditioning,' observed the Abbot.

'Extravagant expenditure, aimed at improving personal comfort, is hardly appropriate in our walk of life,' Sister Grace replied. 'I was reluctant to have money spent on painkillers during my recent illness, but the Mother Superior insisted on it.'

The Abbot regarded such an attitude as way over the top. Had she any idea how hot it had been in his car? 'Have you been able to play any bridge since your illness?' he enquired.

'Not yet,' Sister Grace replied. 'I can partner you tonight in our duplicate if you like.' She felt duty-bound to make such an offer. No other nun would welcome an evening opposite the Abbot.

A few hours later, the game was under way.

```
Both Vul.              ♠ A Q J 6 4
Dealer West            ♡ A K 5
                       ◇ A 6 3
                       ♣ 8 2
        ♠ K 10 9 8 7 3 2       N        ♠ —
        ♡ J 7                           ♡ Q 10 9 6 4
        ◇ 10 8 7       W        E       ◇ K Q J 5
        ♣ 6                  S          ♣ 9 7 5 3
                       ♠ 5
                       ♡ 8 3 2
                       ◇ 9 4 2
                       ♣ A K Q J 10 4
```

WEST	NORTH	EAST	SOUTH
Sister	*Sister*	*Sister*	*The*
Euphemia	*Grace*	*Frances*	*Abbot*
2◇	Dble	Pass	5♣
All Pass			

Sister Euphemia opened with a multi 2♦ and the Abbot ended in 5♣. The ♠10 was led and down went the dummy.

Now, thought the Abbot, which major suit was West likely to hold? It seemed right to finesse the spade queen, anyway.

The homely Sister Frances ruffed the ♠Q and returned the ♦K. The Abbot ducked this trick, hoping that some squeeze would develop later. He won the next diamond and drew trumps in four rounds. He continued with a heart to the ace and the ♠A, discarding a heart. Finally he ruffed a spade and played his remaining trumps. East held the sole guard in hearts but West's ♦10 guarded the other red suit. The contract was one down.

'A bit careless at Trick 1, Hugo,' Sister Grace remarked.

The Abbot blinked. Trick 1? What did she mean?

'You should play low twice, ruffing the second round,' Sister Grace continued, 'then you can score two tricks with the ♠A-Q-J, throwing three losers. Still, it wasn't easy for you.'

'I didn't miss any such plays in the Bermuda Bowl,' replied the Abbot. 'It was just a momentary lapse after the long journey.'

On the next round two noticeably overweight nuns arrived. Sister Myrtle smiled brightly at the Abbot. 'May I offer you a nut toffee?' she asked.

'I have already dined,' replied the Abbot, sorting his cards for the first board of the round:

Both Vul.
Dealer North

	♠ K 6 4 2	
	♡ 10 9 6 5 3	
	◇ K Q	
	♣ J 3	
♠ Q J 10 9 7		♠ A
♡ A	N	♡ 7 4
◇ 10 8 4 2	W E	◇ 9 7 6 5 3
♣ Q 5 2	S	♣ 10 9 8 6 4
	♠ 8 5 3	
	♡ K Q J 8 2	
	◇ A J	
	♣ A K 7	

WEST	NORTH	EAST	SOUTH
Sister	*Sister*	*Sister*	*The*
Myrtle	*Grace*	*Benedict*	*Abbot*
–	Pass	Pass	1♡
Pass	4♡	All Pass	

Sister Myrtle unwrapped a toffee for herself and led the ♠Q.

'Play low,' said the Abbot. He permitted himself a small smile when the ♠A appeared from East. Most of the present field would call for dummy's ♠K at trick 1, hopeless play as that was. He won the club return and played two rounds of diamonds, followed by the ♣K and a club ruff. With these preparations behind him, he led a trump.

West won with the ♡A and persisted with the ♠J, covered by the king and ruffed by Sister Benedict. She was forced to return a minor suit, conceding a ruff-and-discard, and the Abbot disposed of his remaining spade loser. Dummy play of the highest order! Perhaps one of the opponents would have a kind word to say.

'I didn't want a club back, partner,' exclaimed Sister Myrtle. 'Come over to my ace of trumps instead and you won't have to give a ruff-and-discard when you take your spade ruff.'

'I don't see how she's meant to find a trump return,' Sister Grace observed. 'Everyone else will make it, don't worry.'

On the next round, the Abbot's opponents were two fresh-faced novices, who had entered the convent only two months before.

East-West Vul.
Dealer North

	♠ 7 5 4	
	♡ Q 10 2	
	◇ A 5	
	♣ A J 9 6 3	
♠ K Q 2		♠ A 9 8 3
♡ 4	N	♡ K 9 7 5
◇ 10 9 8 4 2	W E	◇ K Q J 3
♣ 10 8 5 4	S	♣ 2
	♠ J 10 6	
	♡ A J 8 6 3	
	◇ 7 6	
	♣ K Q 7	

WEST	NORTH	EAST	SOUTH
Sister	*Sister*	*Sister*	*The*
Chloë	*Grace*	*Imogen*	*Abbot*
–	1♣	Dble	1♡
Pass	2♡	Pass	4♡
All Pass			

The blonde-haired Sister Chloë smiled nervously at the Abbot and led the ♠K. Her partner's ♠9 was high enough to encourage a continuation of the ♠Q and a third round of the suit went to East's

♠A. The Abbot won the ♢K switch in dummy and ran the ♡Q successfully. 'And the ten of trumps,' he said.

Sister Imogen, who was unusually tall for a 15-year-old, covered with the trump king. The Abbot won with the ace and West discarded a diamond. What now? He would need to enter dummy for a trump finesse and then return to score some more club tricks.

The Abbot soon spotted the required play. He led the ♣K and overtook with dummy's ace. A marked finesse of the ♡8 came next and he drew East's last trump with the jack. When he played the ♣Q, he was happy to see East show out. Yes indeed, his expert play in the club suit had been necessary. What a valuable lesson for these two young girls!

The Abbot finessed the ♣9, threw his diamond loser on the ♣J and ten tricks were there. Sister Grace bent forward to fill out the score-sheet. 'Average board,' she reported.

The Abbot had been hoping for better news. 'Really?' he said.

'The Mother Superior is Pair 1,' Sister Grace replied. 'She made eleven tricks on a diamond lead. Two losers go on the clubs then.'

'I'd never lead a diamond,' declared Sister Chloë. 'Partner's likely to hold the ♠A when she doubles a heart opening.'

'I wonder if you could have beaten it,' continued Sister Grace, looking at the curtain cards. 'What happens if Imogen returns a fourth round of spades? Ah, Chloë only had a singleton ♡4. You'd have had to ruff in your hand with the ♡6, Hugo, otherwise the ♡4 knocks out an honour from dummy and promotes a trump trick for East.'

'That was my plan,' replied the Abbot learnedly.

A few rounds later, the Abbot faced two middle-aged nuns. No doubt they played the same sort of game as most of the monks back at St Titus – wooden, unimaginative and very moderate in the card play depart-ment. Still, it wasn't their fault. Only the chosen few could be truly world-class.

This was the deal before them:

East-West Vul.   ♠ K 9 6 4
Dealer East   ♡ K 5
         ♢ A Q J 9 5
         ♣ A J

  ♠ 8   ♠ 10
  ♡ 9 8 6 4   ♡ A Q J 7 2
  ♢ 6 2   ♢ K 8 7 3
  ♣ Q 10 9 7 6 3   ♣ K 8 4

       ♠ A Q J 7 5 3 2
       ♡ 10 3
       ♢ 10 4
       ♣ 5 2

WEST	NORTH	EAST	SOUTH
The	*Sister*	*Sister*	*Sister*
Abbot	*Maud*	*Grace*	*Jubila*
–	–	1♡	3♠
Pass	4♠	All Pass	

The Abbot led the ♡9. 'Better try the king,' instructed Sister Jubila. Sister Grace won with the ace and scored a second trick with her queen. What should she do next?

Declarer presumably held seven trump tricks and would shortly add a number of diamond tricks. The only hope for the defence was to set up a club trick that could be cashed when the diamond finesse lost.

Sister Grace was about to switch to a low club when a thought occurred to her. Suppose the Abbot did produce the ♣Q, won with dummy's ace. Declarer could then run all her trumps, reducing the East hand to the ♢K-8 and ♣K. A club exit would then force her in to lead into dummy's ♢A-Q.

There were only four or five nuns in the convent capable of such a throw-in play and Sister Jubila was not among them. Still, there was no harm in defending accurately. Hugo had presumably played well in Chennai. She would show him that her own play was not too rusty. Sister Grace placed the ♣K on the table.

Sister Jubila won with dummy's ace, drew trumps and ran the ♢10. A diamond and a club trick put the game one down.

'I needed the diamond finesse to work,' observed Sister Jubila. 'We were unlucky in both the red suits, partner.'

It was not Sister Maud's habit to follow the play when she was dummy. She opened the score-sheet and entered the result with a resigned air. 'Everyone else made it,' she said. 'Still, never mind.'

In the last round of the session, the Abbot faced the ancient Mother of Discipline, much feared by the convent's novices. Her black punishment book was clearly visible under her scorecard. Unusually, during the present session, she had not yet found any cause to use it.

'Hugo has recently returned from abroad,' said Sister Grace speaking loudly for the Mother of Discipline's benefit. 'His team came tenth in the Bermuda Bowl.'

The Mother of Discipline surveyed the Abbot disapprovingly. 'Not all of us have the time for bridge holidays in the Caribbean,' she declared. 'Not to mention the extravagant waste of money that could have been devoted to the poor and the suffering. Have you no sense of duty towards your community?'

'It wasn't a holiday,' replied the Abbot. 'The Bermuda Bowl is a major championship with the best players in the world. It was held in Chennai.'

The Mother of Discipline reached for her cards. 'Hardly worth going all the way to the Caribbean just to finish tenth,' she said.

This was the deal before them:

East-West Vul.
Dealer East

	♠ K Q 9 2	
	♡ Q 8 4 3	
	◇ 8 6	
	♣ A Q 4	
♠ 8	N	♠ 4
♡ 9 6	W　E	♡ A K J 10 5 2
◇ K 10 9 5 4 3	S	◇ Q J 7
♣ 10 9 8 6		♣ K J 2
	♠ A J 10 7 6 5 3	
	♡ 7	
	◇ A 2	
	♣ 7 5 3	

WEST	NORTH	EAST	SOUTH
Sister	*Mother of*	*The*	*Mother*
Grace	*Discipline*	*Abbot*	*Superior*
–	–	1♡	1♠
Pass	2♡	Dble	3♠
Pass	4♠	All Pass	

Sister Grace led the ♡9 and the Mother of Discipline deposited her dummy on the table. The Mother Superior leaned forward to arrange the cards into neat lines. 'Nice hand, Reverend Mother.'

Since it would not suit her for the ♡9 to win the trick, allowing West to switch to a club, the Mother Superior called for the ♡Q at Trick 1.

The Abbot won with the king and switched to the ♢Q, declarer winning with the ace.

The Mother Superior crossed to the ♠K, all following, and led the ♡8. As she knew from the opening lead, only the Abbot could beat this card. When he covered with the ♡10, she discarded the diamond loser from her hand. She ruffed the diamond continuation, crossed to the ♠9 and ruffed another heart in her hand. A trump to the queen left these cards still in play:

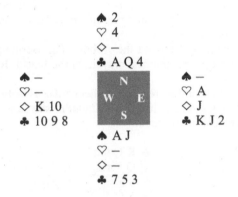

The Mother Superior smiled warmly at the Abbot. 'I think you know what's coming next, Hugo,' she said. 'Play the heart.'

Trying to look as if he were enjoying the moment, the Abbot won with the ♡A. When declarer discarded a club from her hand, he returned the ♢J. The Mother Superior disposed of her remaining club loser and ruffed in the dummy. The game was hers. 'Don't tell me that the ♣K was onside all along!' she said.

'I'm afraid not,' said Sister Grace, displaying her ♣10-9-8.

'You had a sequence in clubs?' queried the Abbot. 'A club lead through the ace-queen beats it.'

'I suppose I might have found a club lead without your double of Two Hearts,' replied Sister Grace.

'Foolish double!' muttered the Mother of Discipline, moving the next board into position. 'The sort of thing they do on bridge holidays, no doubt.'

This was the final board of the session:

Both Vul.
Dealer West

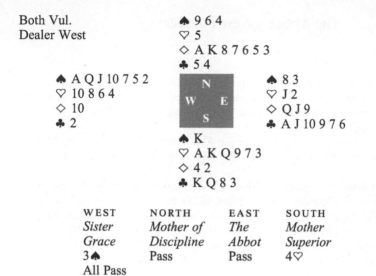

	♠ 9 6 4
	♡ 5
	◇ A K 8 7 6 5 3
	♣ 5 4

♠ A Q J 10 7 5 2
♡ 10 8 6 4
◇ 10
♣ 2

♠ 8 3
♡ J 2
◇ Q J 9
♣ A J 10 9 7 6

♠ K
♡ A K Q 9 7 3
◇ 4 2
♣ K Q 8 3

WEST	NORTH	EAST	SOUTH
Sister	*Mother of*	*The*	*Mother*
Grace	*Discipline*	*Abbot*	*Superior*
3♠	Pass	Pass	4♡
All Pass			

Sister Grace led the ♣2 and the Abbot won with the ace. There was no point in returning a spade, since declarer was marked with a singleton. The Abbot returned the ♣J, covered with the king.

Sister Grace ruffed and played the ♠A, dropping declarer's king. The defence could make no further tricks. The Mother Superior won the diamond switch in dummy and played six rounds of trumps. On the last round the Abbot had to discard from the ◇Q-J and the ♣10-9. Resignedly he threw a club and the Mother Superior then claimed the ♣Q-8 and a diamond to make the game.

'Was that right, Hugo, rising with the ♣A?' queried Sister Grace. 'You could see that it would set up declarer's king-queen. I'm not sure the Reverend Mother can make it if you play the ♣9 instead.'

'I think you're right,' said the Mother Superior. 'Suppose I win with the ♣Q, draw three rounds of trumps, cross to a diamond and lead a club towards the king. Hugo can rise with the ace and lead another diamond for you to ruff. I would still have to lose a spade and a club.'

'Or he could just play another middle club on the second round,' continued Sister Grace. 'You still can't make it.'

'Should have beaten it, should he?' muttered the Mother of Discipline. 'No wonder he only came tenth on his bridge holiday!'

15.   The Abbot's New Partner

On the first Friday of the month, it was the Mother of Discipline's custom to attend the novice duplicate. She was somewhat distressed to hear that her regular partner for this task, Sister Grace, had been restricted to her bed.

'Perhaps you could partner the Abbot instead,' suggested the Mother Superior. 'He may be able to offer some useful tips to our young players.'

'I doubt it,' replied the Mother of Discipline. 'From what I saw of his play on Wednesday, they're more likely to pick up some bad habits.'

The noisy chatter in the novice's cardroom hushed immediately as the stooped figure of the Mother of Discipline entered, followed by the Abbot. 'Take your seats, girls!' she said. Play began and this was an early board:

```
Neither Vul.              ♠ 9 5 3
Dealer North              ♡ A 5
                          ◇ K J 8 7 5
                          ♣ A 6 3
        ♠ K 10                              ♠ Q 8 7
        ♡ 8 3 2            N                ♡ J 10 6
        ◇ 9 6 4 3      W       E            ◇ A Q 10
        ♣ K Q J 4          S                ♣ 10 8 7 5
                          ♠ A J 6 4 2
                          ♡ K Q 9 7 4
                          ◇ 2
                          ♣ 9 2
```

WEST	NORTH	EAST	SOUTH
Sister	*The*	*Sister*	*Mother of*
Colleen	*Abbot*	*Yvette*	*Discipline*
–	1◇	Pass	1♠
Pass	2♠	Pass	4♠
All Pass			

Looking somewhat ill-at-ease in the presence of two such senior players, Sister Colleen led the ♣K. The Abbot attempted a warm smile at his partner as he laid out his dummy.

'By the blessed Saint Odhran!' cried the Mother of Discipline.

Sister Colleen's mouth fell open. 'Was I not meant to lead a club, Reverend Mother?'

'Be silent, foolish child,' remonstrated the Mother of Discipline. 'I am referring to my partner's senseless bidding. How can spades be raised on such a hand?'

The Abbot raised his eyebrows. 'You prefer four-card support?'

'Since my response shows only four cards, of course you need four for a raise,' came the reply. 'Does 4 plus 3 equal 8 at the Monastery of St Titus? What an appalling example to set for these young girls.'

In truth, the Abbot was almost as terrified of the Mother of Discipline as the novices were. He refrained from further comment and the play proceeded. After winning the club lead with dummy's ace, the elderly declarer continued with three top hearts. The suit broke 3-3 and she ditched a club from dummy. Without touching the trump suit, she then played a fourth round of hearts. If West allowed her partner to ruff this trick, dummy's last club would disappear. Ace and another trump would pick up the defenders' trumps subsequently and declarer would lose only two trump tricks and the ◇A.

Hoping that her defence would escape criticism, Sister Colleen ruffed with the ♠10. The Mother of Discipline pointed at dummy's last club, directing the Abbot to dispose of it. She ruffed the ♣Q continuation in dummy and played a trump to her ace, dropping West's king. A trump to dummy's bare nine forced East's queen and declarer was soon able to draw the last trump and claim the contract.

'You played it well,' said the Abbot, hoping to restore normal relations with his obstreperous partner.

'A very lucky lie of the cards,' retorted the Mother of Discipline. 'The bidding didn't deserve to be rewarded in that way. I was hoping to go down.'

The Abbot had been looking for an opportunity to display his own skills at the game. Perhaps this would draw an admiring glance or two from the novices, some of whom were rather pretty. A couple of rounds later, he picked up a balanced hand containing two queens and a jack. What magic was he expected to create with that?

North-South Vul.
Dealer South

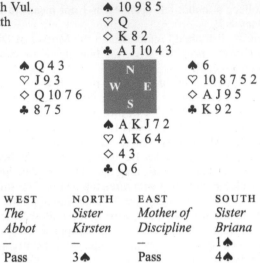

```
                    ♠ 10 9 8 5
                    ♡ Q
                    ◇ K 8 2
                    ♣ A J 10 4 3
    ♠ Q 4 3                        ♠ 6
    ♡ J 9 3                        ♡ 10 8 7 5 2
    ◇ Q 10 7 6                     ◇ A J 9 5
    ♣ 8 7 5                        ♣ K 9 2
                    ♠ A K J 7 2
                    ♡ A K 6 4
                    ◇ 4 3
                    ♣ Q 6
```

WEST	NORTH	EAST	SOUTH
The	*Sister*	*Mother of*	*Sister*
Abbot	*Kirsten*	*Discipline*	*Briana*
–	–	–	1♠
Pass	3♠	Pass	4♠
All Pass			

The Abbot led the ◇6 and the blonde-haired Sister Kirsten laid out her dummy somewhat nervously. Was a raise to the three-level the right move on her hand? If not, she would soon find out!

When the Mother of Discipline remained silent, Sister Kirsten felt able to relax again. It was now poor Sister Briana who would have to watch her step. Woe betide her if she made some stupid play against this particular opponent.

'King, please,' said Sister Briana.

The Mother of Discipline won with the ace and returned the ◇5 to the Abbot's ◇10. The young declarer ruffed the third round of diamonds and played two top trumps. She sighed when East showed out on the second round. Was it her fault if the trumps happened to break badly? Oh dear, to make the contract now she would need the club finesse to succeed. No such luck was forthcoming and the game went one down.

'Appalling play!' snapped the Mother of Discipline.

'But three finesses were wrong, Reverend Mother,' protested Sister Briana. 'That's not my fault.'

The Mother of Discipline reached for her black punishment book. 'That will be one day on Saint Iona's regime,' she announced, making a note to this effect. 'How many times have I told you to think at Trick 1? Did you think that Abbot Hugo here is so foolish as to lead away from the ◇A?'

Sister Briana glanced at the Abbot. 'I don't expect so, Reverend Mother, but it was my only chance to avoid losing a trick in the suit.'

'Stupid girl!' exclaimed the Mother of Discipline. 'Cover the ◇6 with dummy's ◇8 and the contract is yours. If I cash the ◇A after winning with the ◇J, you will have a discard for your club loser. If I don't, you can discard dummy's remaining diamonds on your top hearts.'

All memory of the deal had fled from the novice's mind. 'That's very clever, Reverend Mother,' she said.

'It's entirely obvious,' continued the Mother of Discipline. 'If you can't get to sleep tonight without a pillow, remember two things. Firstly, Saint Iona slept without a pillow, in great discomfort, through-out her adult life. Secondly, you should always think before playing to Trick 1. If you find it difficult to eat your cereal without milk tomorrow morning, remember two more things. Firstly that Saint Iona never took milk with her cereal and lived with a perpetual sore throat as a result. Secondly, that it is rarely right to play an unsupported king from dummy at Trick 1.'

'Yes, indeed, Reverend Mother,' Sister Briana replied. 'The blessed saint is an inspiring example to us all.'

'Had Saint Iona played bridge, I dare say she would have led the queen or ten of diamonds from your hand, Hugo,' declared the Mother of Discipline. 'That gives the contract no chance at all.'

With some difficulty the Abbot refrained from comment. For a moment he wondered if the Mother of Discipline was related to Brother Xavier. Such double-dummy opening lead suggestions were right up his street. At least his low diamond lead had beaten the contract. Who in the world would even think of leading the queen or ten from such a combination?

The Mother of Discipline entered the result in her scorecard. 'No chance at all,' she muttered.

Soon afterwards the Abbot faced two minuscule 15-year-olds. He looked at them with some concern. They could hardly weigh more than 7 stone each! What sort of diet had the Mother of Discipline enforced on them? On closer inspection, it seemed that they might be twins. They were both wearing identical metal-rimmed spectacles.

'Good evening, Reverend Mother,' chanted the newcomers in unison. 'We hope you're having an enjoyable session.'

The Mother of Discipline beckoned for the play to start. This was the first board of the round:

East-West Vul.   ♠ 8 6 5 3 2
Dealer South   ♡ Q 7
                ◇ A K 6 5
                ♣ 7 2

♠ A	**N**	♠ 9 4
♡ 10 6 4 3	**W E**	♡ 8 5 2
◇ 10 8 7 2	**S**	◇ Q J 9 3
♣ K Q J 8		♣ 10 6 5 4

                ♠ K Q J 10 7
                ♡ A K J 9
                ◇ 4
                ♣ A 9 3

WEST	NORTH	EAST	SOUTH
The	*Sister*	*Mother of*	*Sister*
Abbot	*Shauna*	*Discipline*	*Brigid*
–	–	–	1♠
Pass	4♠	Pass	4NT
Pass	5◇	Pass	6♠
All Pass			

Hoping that his opening lead might evade subsequent criticism, the Abbot placed the ♣K on the table. Sister Brigid won with the ♣A and noted that she now had two top losers. The Mother of Discipline had been known to lose her temper when a novice didn't draw trumps immediately, but here it seemed that it might be a mistake.

Fearful as she was of bringing the Black Punishment Book into action, Sister Brigid decided to play on hearts before drawing trumps. She played the queen, ace and king of hearts, discarding dummy's last club as both defenders followed suit. With a second loser avoided, she then played a trump.

The Abbot won with the trump ace and promptly returned a fourth round of hearts. Sister Brigid surveyed this card with some alarm. 'Ruff with the eight, please, partner,' she said.

An overruff with the ♠9 put the slam one down.

'Unbelievable carelessness!' exclaimed the Mother of Discipline. 'Pride comes before a fall, girl. You were so busy preening yourself after your play in hearts, you totally lost concentration.'

Sister Brigid bowed her head, staring at the baize as she awaited her fate.

'How can you leave the ♡J in your hand?' persisted the Mother of Discipline. 'You should play the ace and king of diamonds, discarding the last heart. Then you draw trumps. That's the way to play it.'

Sister Brigid saw a small chance to avoid punishment. 'What a wonderful play, Reverend Mother!' she declared. 'I'll never be able to play as well as you do.'

'True enough,' mumbled the Mother of Discipline. 'Still, we must strive our utmost to achieve what we can in this life.'

'Wise words, Reverend Mother,' said Sister Shauna. 'We're both so grateful for your help with our play.'

The Mother of Discipline tapped her fingers on the table, eventually deciding that no punishment would be necessary on this occasion. It was good to know that her efforts to help the girls were appreciated.

On the last round the Abbot faced the two best players in the novitiate. It would soon be time for their Temporary Profession of Vows and this was one of the last times they would play in the novices' duplicate. This was the deal before them:

Both Vul.
Dealer East

```
                    ♠ 4 2
                    ♡ 10 9 6 3
                    ◇ K 9 7
                    ♣ A K Q J
    ♠ 5 3                           ♠ Q J 10 9 6
    ♡ J 5 4 2          N            ♡ A
    ◇ Q 10 2      W        E        ◇ A J 8 4
    ♣ 8 6 4 3         S            ♣ 10 5 2
                    ♠ A K 8 7
                    ♡ K Q 8 7
                    ◇ 6 5 3
                    ♣ 9 7
```

WEST	NORTH	EAST	SOUTH
Mother of	*Sister*	*The*	*Sister*
Discipline	*Ailionora*	*Abbot*	*Kiara*
–	–	1♠	Pass
Pass	Dble	Pass	2♠
Pass	3♣	Pass	3♡
Pass	4♡	All Pass	

The Mother of Discipline led the ♠5, the dark-haired Sister Kiara winning with the ace. A club to dummy was followed by a round of trumps, the ace appearing from East. Declarer won the spade continuation and played the king of trumps, discovering a second loser in the suit. After drawing a third round with the queen, she played three more rounds of clubs, throwing two diamonds. The lead was in dummy with these cards still in play:

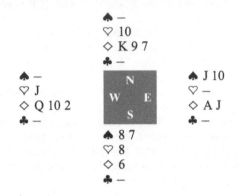

```
              ♠ —
              ♡ 10
              ◇ K 9 7
              ♣ —
♠ —                        ♠ J 10
♡ J           N            ♡ —
◇ Q 10 2    W   E          ◇ A J
♣ —           S            ♣ —
              ♠ 8 7
              ♡ 8
              ◇ 6
              ♣ —
```

Sister Kiara was hoping to score some more trump tricks. With this aim in mind, she called for dummy's ◇K. When the Abbot won with the ace and returned the ◇J, declarer ruffed with the ♡8. She then led a spade towards dummy's ♡10, promoting that card into her tenth trick. The game had been made.

The Abbot could not resist a comment to his partner. 'Lead the queen or ten of diamonds, as you recommended to me a short while ago, and it goes down,' he said. 'In fact it goes two down.'

The Mother of Discipline glared at him. 'Did it not occur to you to make a lead-directing bid of Two Diamonds?' she demanded. For a brief moment an inbuilt reflex caused her to reach towards her Punishment Book. Attempting to disguise this, she picked up her pen and wrote down the score. 'Rebid Two Diamonds over North's double and you change a bottom into a top!'

The session drew to an end and the novices streamed out of the cardroom. The Abbot looked across at his elderly partner, who showed no immediate sign of leaving her chair. 'You were rather harsh with some of the girls, Reverend Mother,' he observed.

The Mother of Discipline looked the Abbot in the eye. 'It's an onerous duty and it pains me deeply to hurt the young dears' feelings,' she replied, rising to her feet with some difficulty. 'Spare the rod and you spoil the child. It's the only way to improve their game!'

16.   The Abbot's Fan Club

The Abbot's last full day at the convent coincided with the visit of Monsignor Agostino, confessor to the nuns. A moderate bridge player, he rarely took part in the convent duplicates. When he heard of the Abbot's presence, however, he was determined to join forces. 'I'm sure we'll do very well together, Abbot,' he said. 'I usually come in the top third at my local club. Mind you, I have a very good partner there.'

Seeing no escape, the Abbot acquiesced. An early round saw the uncertain partnership facing tough opposition:

```
Neither Vul.                ♠ 6 5 3
Dealer South                ♡ A Q 10
                            ◇ K J 8 7
                            ♣ J 9 4
      ♠ K Q J 10 8                        ♠ 2
      ♡ K J 9 7 3          N              ♡ 8 6 5 4
      ◇ 6 4            W        E          ◇ 5 3
      ♣ 3                  S              ♣ 10 8 7 6 5 2
                            ♠ A 9 7 4
                            ♡ 2
                            ◇ A Q 10 9 2
                            ♣ A K Q
```

WEST	NORTH	EAST	SOUTH
The	*Sister*	*Monsignor*	*Mother*
Abbot	*Thomas*	*Agostino*	*Superior*
–	–	–	1◇
2◇	2♡	Pass	2♠
Pass	2NT	Pass	6◇
All Pass			

When the Abbot overcalled 2◇, Sister Thomas turned her bushy eyebrows in the Monsignor's direction. 'What does that mean?' she enquired.

'I've absolutely no idea,' he replied. 'A strong hand?'

The Abbot gritted his teeth. His partner's answer might have made some sense fifty or sixty years ago. Surely, even in the social backwaters that the Monsignor inhabited, Michaels cue-bids were commonly played?

Arriving in 6◇, the Mother Superior won the spade lead and drew trumps in two rounds. She continued to play minor-suit winners, arriving at this position:

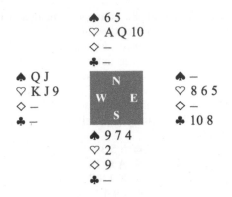

```
              ♠ 6 5
              ♡ A Q 10
              ◇ —
              ♣ —
   ♠ Q J                      ♠ —
   ♡ K J 9         N          ♡ 8 6 5
   ◇ —         W       E      ◇ —
   ♣ —             S          ♣ 10 8
              ♠ 9 7 4
              ♡ 2
              ◇ 9
              ♣ —
```

When the ◇9 appeared from South, the Abbot sat back in his chair.

'In trouble, Hugo?' asked the Mother Superior, raising her eyebrows.

'You played it well,' the Abbot replied, resignedly tossing the ♠J onto the table.

'Small spade from the dummy?' queried Sister Thomas.

'Oh well, just for a little bit of fun you can throw the ♡Q,' replied the Mother Superior. She exited with a spade to the Abbot's queen, won the ♡K return with dummy's ace and claimed the last two tricks with her ♠9-7. The slam had been made.

'Difficult for you, Hugo,' declared the Mother Superior. 'If you happen to lead a heart, you break the link with the dummy.'

'Heart lead, yes,' declared Monsignor Agostino, shaking his head. 'It's amazing how often the wrong lead lets a contract through. My regular partner, Herbert Simmonds, he says that the opening lead is the most important part of the hand.'

The Abbot glanced at his watch. Goodness me, had they only been playing for 20 minutes? It seemed like at least two hours. How entirely clueless his partner was!

Somehow the Abbot restrained himself when the Monsignor subsequently went down in two very makeable contracts, only to place the blame on partner's bidding. His spirits were revived when at long last he picked up a good hand. What was more, he was facing two bright-looking novices who might show some appreciation if he found a noteworthy line of play:

Neither Vul.
Dealer East

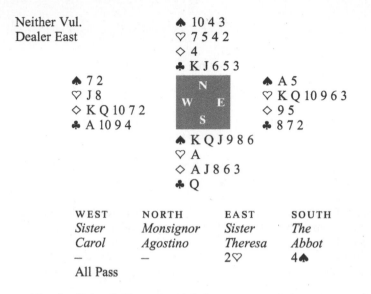

```
                    ♠ 10 4 3
                    ♡ 7 5 4 2
                    ◇ 4
                    ♣ K J 6 5 3
    ♠ 7 2                          ♠ A 5
    ♡ J 8              N           ♡ K Q 10 9 6 3
    ◇ K Q 10 7 2   W     E        ◇ 9 5
    ♣ A 10 9 4         S           ♣ 8 7 2
                    ♠ K Q J 9 8 6
                    ♡ A
                    ◇ A J 8 6 3
                    ♣ Q
```

WEST	NORTH	EAST	SOUTH
Sister	*Monsignor*	*Sister*	*The*
Carol	*Agostino*	*Theresa*	*Abbot*
–	–	2♡	4♠

All Pass

The fresh-faced Sister Carol led a trump and the Monsignor laid down his dummy. 'If you have the ten tricks you promised, we can maybe make a slam,' he observed. 'I have three trumps, a singleton and a useful king for you.'

The two novices looked at the Abbot to see how he would react to this absurd observation. 'You judged it well,' he replied.

Sister Theresa, who had been captain of judo at the Our Lady of Sustenance secondary school, won the first trick with the ace of trumps and returned a trump. The Abbot won in his hand, cashed the ♡A and continued with the ♣Q. Sister Carol could see no future in winning the trick, setting up dummy's ♣K-J for two discards. When a low club appeared from West, the Abbot overtook with dummy's ♣K. It won the trick and he then led a diamond, covering East's ◇5 with the ◇8. Sister Carol won with the ◇10 and exited safely with the ♡J, ruffed by the Abbot.

The Abbot had noted East's ♣2 on the first round, presumably showing three clubs. Her likely shape was 2-6-2-3. She could hardly hold a diamond honour in addition to the points already shown. If her last diamond was the ◇9, he might be in business!

The Abbot led the ◇J from his hand. Sister Carol won with the ◇Q and (yes!) the ◇9 fell from East. He discarded a heart from dummy, leaving West on lead. These cards were still to be played:

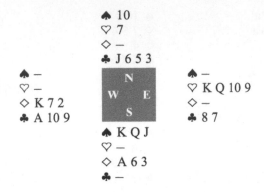

```
              ♠ 10
              ♡ 7
              ◇ —
              ♣ J 6 5 3
♠ —                        ♠ —
♡ —                        ♡ K Q 10 9
◇ K 7 2                    ◇ —
♣ A 10 9                   ♣ 8 7
              ♠ K Q J
              ♡ —
              ◇ A 6 3
              ♣ —
```

Sister Carol could see that a club exit would surrender the contract. The Abbot would be able to ruff one diamond and discard the other on the ♣J. She decided to exit with the ◇7. The Abbot won with the ◇A and led the ◇6 for a ruffing finesse. Sister Carol covered with the ◇K and the Abbot eventually scored his tenth trick with the ◇3 over West's ◇2.

'That was hard work,' reprimanded Monsignor Agostino. 'Did you have your bid, partner? I gave you quite a strong dummy.'

The Abbot suppressed a smile. He had rarely witnessed such an accurate impression of Brother Xavier. Cardplay descended from the very heavens and all he could talk about was the bidding!

Meanwhile, Sister Carol was thinking back over the play. 'Wow, that was amazing,' she exclaimed. 'How did you work it out, setting up the ◇3 like that?'

'I played a very similar hand in the Bermuda Bowl against er . . . India,' the Abbot replied. 'It's surprising what becomes possible if you keep track of the cards and count the hand.'

'No-one here at the convent plays anything like as well as you do,' observed Sister Theresa. 'Do you mind if we take a note of the hand so we can look at it later?'

The Abbot was in ecstasy. Thank goodness there were human beings left on the planet who recognized a good piece of card play when they saw one. 'By all means,' he replied. 'You may have forgotten how the play went. I can go through it with you later if you like.'

Sister Carol's face lit up. 'That would be great!' she said.

The chapel clock was sounding 10 o'clock as the Abbot and the Monsignor arrived at the Mother of Discipline's table. 'Don't forget our meeting tomorrow after Lauds,' she said gruffly.

'Of course not, Reverend Mother,' Monsignor Agostino replied. Whatever the official policy on secrets of the confessional might be, the

Mother of Discipline insisted on keeping track of the indiscretions confessed by her flock of novices.

This was the first board of the round:

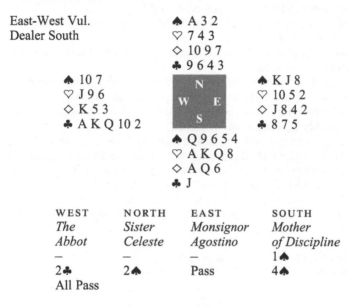

East-West Vul.
Dealer South

♠ A 3 2
♡ 7 4 3
♢ 10 9 7
♣ 9 6 4 3

♠ 10 7
♡ J 9 6
♢ K 5 3
♣ A K Q 10 2

♠ K J 8
♡ 10 5 2
♢ J 8 4 2
♣ 8 7 5

♠ Q 9 6 5 4
♡ A K Q 8
♢ A Q 6
♣ J

WEST	NORTH	EAST	SOUTH
The	*Sister*	*Monsignor*	*Mother*
Abbot	*Celeste*	*Agostino*	*of Discipline*
–	–	–	1♠
2♣	2♠	Pass	4♠
All Pass			

The Abbot led the ♣K and Sister Celeste laid out her dummy as attractively as she could. 'Not much there for me,' muttered the Mother of Discipline.

Sister Celeste smiled cheerfully. 'Ah well, I couldn't pass with the best card in the pack.'

The Mother of Discipline ruffed the club continuation. There was only one entry to dummy and she needed to lose only one trump and one diamond. How could it be done?

One option was to use the ♠A entry to run the ♢10. If this forced West's king, she would then have to hope that the ♠K was doubleton. And that the hearts lay well – it wasn't a good game.

Spotting a better line, the Mother of Discipline led the ♢Q at Trick 3. The Abbot won with the ♢K and forced declarer with another club. Declarer crossed to the ♠A and called for the ♢10. It made no difference whether the Monsignor covered or not. When he covered with the jack, the Mother of Discipline won with the ace and returned to dummy with the ♢9. 'Trump,' she said.

Monsignor Agostino rose with the king of trumps and returned his last trump. Declarer was down to her four hearts. When they split 3-3, the contract was hers.

'I thought it would be there, Reverend Mother,' exclaimed a delighted Sister Celeste. 'You played it well.'

'Another bottom for us!' declared the Monsignor loudly. 'I do much better with my regular partner.'

Several young heads turned. How amusing! The Monsignor was doing badly for some reason.

The Abbot retained his dignity. 'The Reverend Mother played it very well,' he replied. 'There was nothing we could do about it.'

'I would have bid 3♣ on your hand,' continued the Monsignor. 'That would probably keep them out of game.'

For a moment the Abbot checked that this was not some absurd dream. How could a third-rate club player feel entitled to lecture a Bermuda Bowl expert? Overcalling 3♣ would be ludicrous.

'Move for the last round, please!' called a shrill voice.

The Abbot had never heard more welcome words. He took his seat for the final round and was further consoled by picking up a handsome 20-count.

North-South Vul.
Dealer South

```
                    ♠ A Q J 10 9 8 3
                    ♡ 2
                    ◇ 4 2
                    ♣ Q 5 4
   ♠ 7 6 2              N              ♠ 4
   ♡ 10 9 8 5       W       E          ♡ Q J 7 6 4
   ◇ K J 9 5                           ◇ 10 8 7 3
   ♣ 10 8              S               ♣ K J 9
                    ♠ K 5
                    ♡ A K 3
                    ◇ A Q 6
                    ♣ A 7 6 3 2
```

WEST	NORTH	EAST	SOUTH
Sister	*Monsignor*	*Sister*	*The*
Myrtle	*Agostino*	*Benedict*	*Abbot*
–	–	–	2NT
Pass	3♡	Pass	3♠
Pass	6♠	All Pass	

Sister Myrtle led the ♡10 and the Monsignor laid out his dummy. 'I wouldn't normally bid six on this,' he explained. 'We've done so badly, I thought we needed a good one.'

The capacious Sister Myrtle unwrapped a Sharp's treacle toffee, popping it into her mouth. 'You could have been missing two aces, Monsignor,' she said. 'Aren't you playing Blackwood? It's very useful.'

Sister Benedict nodded her agreement. 'It's unusual to play transfer responses and not Blackwood.'

Ignoring this inane chatter, the Abbot paused to make a plan. Suppose he won and played a club to the queen. If this lost to East's king, she would doubtless switch to a diamond. With the ◇A gone, he would no longer be able to discard a club on the ♡A, ruff the clubs good and get back to the long cards. Not unless trumps were 2-2, anyway.

'Shall I play the ♡2?' queried the Monsignor.

Perhaps there was a way to set up the clubs without allowing East on lead, thought the Abbot. Ah, of course. How had he missed it? 'Yes, play the ♡2,' he said.

When the Abbot followed with the ♡3 from his hand, the Monsignor flopped backwards in his chair. 'That's all we need,' he exclaimed. 'You can't beat the ♡10?'

The Abbot won the trump switch in dummy, crossed to the ♣A and discarded two clubs on his ♡A-K. A club ruff with the ♠9 was followed by a trump to the king and a further club ruff. It remained only to draw trumps and re-enter his hand with the ◇A to enjoy the established cards in clubs.

'Beautifully played, Hugo!' exclaimed a female voice.

The Abbot spun round to see the pale figure of Sister Grace, wearing a utilitarian grey dressing gown that had seen better days. 'It's wonderful to see you,' he said. 'Are you sure you should be out of bed?'

'I'm so glad I came,' Sister Grace replied. 'Otherwise I'd have missed your play on this hand. Mind you, I am feeling rather weak. Perhaps I should return to my room.'

The Abbot rose to his feet, suddenly feeling a great warmth towards his cousin. 'Let me help you upstairs, my dear,' he said. 'We only have one more board to play. I'm sure the others won't mind waiting a few minutes.'

Part IV A Flying Visit

17.   The Parrot's Long Journey

The Abbot had been looking forward all week to the arrival of a very special guest. He had invited the Parrot, his partner in the Bermuda Bowl, to visit the monastery. The arrangements for his journey had been left to the Upper Bhumpopo missionaries.

'I thought you were expecting him around seven o'clock,' observed Brother Lucius. 'I hope he hasn't got lost.'

'I'll have to stay up all night, if necessary,' replied the Abbot. 'I must be able to welcome him properly. He doesn't know it but I've bought a large carton of his favourite birdseed mixture. It was a special offer on the internet.'

The other monks had all retired for the night when the Abbot heard a weak tapping noise on the monastery's oak front door. He swung it open to reveal a sad sight. The Parrot, his feathers drenched, lay exhausted on the doormat.

'My poor fellow,' exclaimed the Abbot. 'What on earth happened?'

'Brother Tobias bought cheap air ticket,' replied the Parrot, hopping across the threshold. 'Three stopovers and I missed the final Ryanair connection. I had to fly here myself from Hamburg.'

'Let me get you a drink and some birdseed,' replied the Abbot. 'Was the weather bad coming over the English Channel?'

'Freezing!' shrieked the Parrot. He looked around at the dimly lit stone walls. It didn't seem much warmer now that he had arrived.

'I've set up a perch for you in our main laundry cupboard,' said the Abbot. 'It's very warm in there. You'll be fine by the morning.'

The following evening, the Abbot partnered the Parrot in the evening duplicate. The first round brought Brother Aelred and Brother Michael to the Abbot's table.

'I'm very pleased to meet you,' said Brother Aelred, uncertain whether he should offer to shake the Parrot's claw. 'How on earth did you put up with the Abbot as your partner, over in India?'

'Not easy, not easy!' replied the Parrot.

'Well, of course, I was only joking,' continued Brother Aelred. 'Over here we call it the English sense of humour.'

'I see,' said the Parrot. 'Is it funny?'

'Well, yes,' said Brother Aelred. 'We like to think so, anyway.'

Not in the least entertained by this fruitless exchange, the Abbot directed the other players' attention to the board before them:

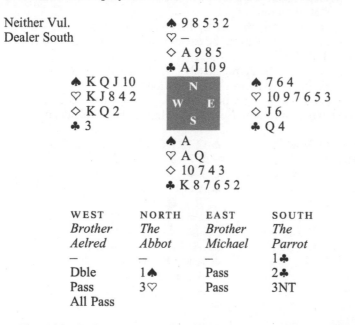

Neither Vul.
Dealer South

♠ 9 8 5 3 2
♡ —
◇ A 9 8 5
♣ A J 10 9

♠ K Q J 10
♡ K J 8 4 2
◇ K Q 2
♣ 3

♠ 7 6 4
♡ 10 9 7 6 5 3
◇ J 6
♣ Q 4

♠ A
♡ A Q
◇ 10 7 4 3
♣ K 8 7 6 5 2

WEST	NORTH	EAST	SOUTH
Brother	*The*	*Brother*	*The*
Aelred	*Abbot*	*Michael*	*Parrot*
—	—	—	1♣
Dble	1♠	Pass	2♣
Pass	3♡	Pass	3NT
All Pass			

The Abbot's 3♡ was a splinter bid, agreeing clubs, and Brother Aelred led the ♠K against the resultant 3NT. When the dummy went down, the Parrot immediately spotted a small problem. Unless the ♣Q fell singleton, the club suit would be blocked. What could be done?

Aiming to unblock two of dummy's high cards in clubs, the Parrot led the ♡Q from his hand at Trick 2. Brother Aelred won with the king and the Parrot threw the ♣9 from dummy. When Brother Aelred cashed a spade trick, the Parrot discarded a diamond. Should he cash two more spades now? Since this would set up the ♠9 in dummy, which might be declarer's ninth trick, he decided to switch to the ◇K instead. 'Ace!' squawked the Parrot. 'And the ace of clubs.'

The ♣Q did not fall but this caused no problem at all. The Parrot returned to his hand with the ♣K and discarded the blocking ♣J on the ♡A. He then scored four more club tricks in his hand, claiming +400.

Brother Aelred was somewhat mystified by the Parrot's line of play. 'Isn't it easier in Five Clubs?' he enquired.

'Of course, of course,' replied the Parrot.

'There's no need to look at me like that,' declared the Abbot. 'I showed you what I had and you chose to play in 3NT. Take away West's obvious spade lead from a sequence and a heart lead would have given us +430 for a top.'

A few rounds later, Brother Cameron took his seat at the Abbot's table. 'Ah, the famous Parrot,' he exclaimed. 'How on earth did you do so well in India?'

The Abbot eyed the Parrot closely. Would it kill him to make some kind remark about his partner's contribution?

'Both played well, both played well,' replied the Parrot, sensing what was expected of him. He extracted his cards for this deal:

North-South Vul.
Dealer West

```
                          ♠ Q 10 7 6
                          ♡ 8 7 4 2
                          ◇ 7 4
                          ♣ A Q J
   ♠ 9                                      ♠ 4
   ♡ K J 10            N                     ♡ Q 6
   ◇ K J 10 9 5 3    W   E                   ◇ Q 8 6
   ♣ K 9 6             S                     ♣ 10 8 7 5 4 3 2
                          ♠ A K J 8 5 3 2
                          ♡ A 9 5 3
                          ◇ A 2
                          ♣ —
```

WEST	NORTH	EAST	SOUTH
The	*Brother*	*The*	*Brother*
Abbot	*Damien*	*Parrot*	*Cameron*
1◇	Pass	Pass	4♠
Pass	5♣	Pass	6♠
All Pass			

The Abbot turned towards Brother Cameron. 'The 5♣ bid?'

'Cue-bid, presumably,' Brother Cameron replied.

The Abbot had no intention of making a suicidal lead from a king. He led the ♠9, won with dummy's ♠10. Brother Cameron continued with the ♣A and ♣Q, throwing two hearts. The Abbot won with the ♣K and exited safely with another club, Brother Cameron discarding his last spot-card in hearts.

After playing the ♡A, Brother Cameron crossed to dummy with the ♠10 and ♠7 to ruff two more hearts in his hand. He then crossed to the ♠Q and discarded his diamond loser on the ♡8, claiming the slam. The Parrot rocked backwards and forwards, a sign of disapproval.

'Surely you don't expect me to lead from a king?' demanded the Abbot. 'How do I know that you've got a red queen?'

'I had both red queens!' exclaimed the Parrot.

'Well, I can't help that,' said the Abbot. 'Perhaps you should have found some response in that case.'

Not long afterwards the Abbot and the Parrot faced Brother Fabius and the black-bearded Brother Zac.

'I've never played bridge against a bird before,' observed Brother Zac as he took his seat. 'I've been looking forward to it.'

The Parrot was tempted to reply that he had never played bridge against someone with a beard so seriously in need of a trim. He managed to restrain himself and sorted his cards for this deal:

```
East-West Vul.           ♠ 6
Dealer East              ♡ A 8 7 5 3
                         ◇ J 6 3
                         ♣ Q J 6 2
        ♠ 9 5 3              N           ♠ 7 2
        ♡ J 10 2        W        E       ♡ K Q 9 6 4
        ◇ K 9 5                          ◇ A 10 8
        ♣ 10 8 7 5           S           ♣ A 9 3
                         ♠ A K Q J 10 8 4
                         ♡ –
                         ◇ Q 7 4 2
                         ♣ K 4
```

WEST	NORTH	EAST	SOUTH
Brother	*The*	*Brother*	*The*
Fabius	*Abbot*	*Zac*	*Parrot*
–	–	1♡	4♠
All Pass			

The ♡J was led and the Parrot took only a moment to see how the deal should be played. He ruffed in his hand and drew trumps in three rounds. He then played the ♣K, West showing his count by following with the ♣8. Brother Zac held up on the first round, aiming to keep declarer out of dummy. When a club was played to the queen, he won with the ace and had no good return. A heart or a club would give the Parrot access to dummy and the two tricks needed for game.

When Brother Zac tried his luck with the ◇8 instead, West won with the king and returned a diamond. If East took his ◇A, the Parrot would claim the remaining tricks. When Brother Zac inserted the ◇10, the

Parrot won and led a third round of diamonds, claiming the contract when they divided 3-3.

'Amazing,' exclaimed Brother Zac. 'You never made the ♡A!'

Brother Fabius turned towards the Abbot. 'Wouldn't it be wonderful if we could all play like that?' he said.

The Abbot could not believe the excessive compliments for a simple end-play. Did they not realize that such a line would be automatic for any member of the monastery first team?

On the next round, Lucius and Paulo arrived at the Abbot's table. 'I observe from the travellers that our esteemed guest has been collecting some fine scores tonight,' said Brother Lucius.

The Abbot sighed. Had Lucius failed to notice the fine score he had achieved himself, making 2♠ against Brother Sextus?

Brother Lucius turned towards the Parrot. 'I see you reached 3NT instead of 5♣ on Board 11,' he said. 'They led a spade?'

The Parrot nodded.

'You played the ♡Q to ditch a club?' continued Brother Lucius.

'Obvious play, obvious play!' squawked the Parrot.

Brother Lucius laughed. 'Not to our declarer,' he replied.

The players drew their cards for this board:

North-South Vul.
Dealer West

```
                    ♠ Q 7
                    ♡ Q 9 5 4
                    ◇ 8 5 3 2
                    ♣ A 10 2
     ♠ 4 2                         ♠ 9 6 3
     ♡ A K J 10 3        N         ♡ 8 6 2
     ◇ A Q 10 9      W     E       ◇ 7 6 4
     ♣ K 6              S          ♣ 9 8 5 3
                    ♠ A K J 10 8 5
                    ♡ 7
                    ◇ K J
                    ♣ Q J 7 4
```

WEST	NORTH	EAST	SOUTH
Brother	*The*	*Brother*	*The*
Lucius	*Abbot*	*Paulo*	*Parrot*
1♡	Pass	Pass	2♠
Pass	2NT	Pass	3♣
Pass	4♠	All Pass	

Brother Lucius led the ♡K, his partner signalling an odd number of cards in the suit. The Parrot won the trump switch in his hand and crossed to dummy with the queen of trumps. A diamond to the jack, lost to the queen, Paulo again signalling an odd number of cards. Placing declarer with two diamonds, Lucius continued with the ◇A, followed by the ◇10.

The Parrot ruffed in his hand and drew the last trump. His next move was a club to the ten, which won the trick. The Parrot was close to achieving a complete count of the hand. One more diamond ruff would give him the last piece of information needed.

East showed out on the fourth round of diamonds, marking West with an initial 2-5-4-2 shape. The ♣K must now be bare. The Parrot led the ♣7 from his hand and claimed the contract when the king did indeed appear from Brother Lucius.

'Hot stuff!' exclaimed Brother Lucius. 'With that level of play, you could make good money as a professional partner. In the USA, you might pick up $1000 a day.'

'Could be more,' declared Brother Paulo. 'The top players over there make a fortune.'

The Parrot had stopped rocking from side to side. 'Only got $100 a day in Chennai,' he said.

The Abbot was aghast at the direction the conversation had taken. What would the other monks think if they discovered that he had used a large slice of the James Porteous bequest to fund the Bermuda Bowl venture? It didn't bear thinking about. He might even have to relinquish his post as Abbot.

'Some of the teams had sponsors in Chennai,' said the Abbot. 'Of course the rates in India can't compare with those in the USA. Shall we play the next one?'

The players extracted these cards for the second board of the round:

East-West Vul.　　　　　♠ 5 3
Dealer South　　　　　　♡ 4 2
　　　　　　　　　　　　♢ A 9 7 6
　　　　　　　　　　　　♣ K Q 9 8 2

♠ A 9 4　　　　　　　　　♠ J 10
♡ J 10 9 7　　　　　　　　　　　　♡ A 8 6 5 3
♢ Q 10 4　　　　W　　E　　　　♢ K J 8 5 3
♣ 10 7 5　　　　　　　　　　　　♣ 4

　　　　　　　　　　　　♠ K Q 8 7 6 2
　　　　　　　　　　　　♡ K Q
　　　　　　　　　　　　♢ 2
　　　　　　　　　　　　♣ A J 6 3

WEST	NORTH	EAST	SOUTH
Brother	*The*	*Brother*	*The*
Lucius	*Abbot*	*Paulo*	*Parrot*
–	–	–	1♠
Pass	1NT	Pass	3♠
Pass	4♠	All Pass	

Brother Paulo won the ♡J lead with the ace, the queen falling from declarer. The Parrot won the ♣4 return in dummy and called for a trump. The ♠10 appeared on his right and he paused to consider the situation. East's club switch was likely to be a singleton. What would happen if he covered with the ♠K now and East had started with ♠10-9 doubleton? Lucius would win with the ♠A and give Paulo a club ruff with the ♠9. His remaining ♠J-4 would still be worth a trick and that would be one down. The Parrot saw he would fare no better by playing a low trump from his hand. West would still be able to overtake with ♠J and give East a club ruff.

A more interesting case was when East had started with ♠J-10 doubleton. Yes, then he could see a winning play!

The Parrot followed with a low trump and the defence was at an end. Whether or not West overtook with the ♠A and delivered a ruff, the defenders would score only two trump tricks. Lucius allowed the ♠10 to win and East returned a heart. The Parrot won and played the ♠K, soon claiming the contract.

'Nice play in the trump suit,' said Brother Lucius.

'Everyone play it same way,' replied the Parrot modestly. He looked across the table, where the Abbot was stifling a yawn. 'Well, nearly everyone.'

18. The Parrot's Brilliant Lead

'The Winchester green-point Swiss is on Sunday,' said Brother Xavier. 'I hope we do better than last year.'

'Oh, er . . . yes,' replied the Abbot. 'Well, I'm sure you understand but I'll be partnering the Parrot on Sunday. He's only with us for another week and I could hardly leave him at the monastery while we're off enjoying ourselves.'

'When were you planning to tell me?' said Brother Xavier, not looking too pleased at the arrangement.

'I had to enrol the Parrot in the English Bridge Union,' the Abbot replied. 'He says he's 9 but they charged the full adult rate.'

A few days later, the event began in the Winchester Sports Centre. The first round saw the Abbot facing a team from Andover.

'I'm not very happy being watched by a parrot,' declared Emily Glassover, taking her seat. 'I didn't think pets were allowed.'

Before the Parrot could blow his top, the Abbot leaned forward. 'My partner is an expert bridge player,' he informed the opponents. 'We played together in the recent Bermuda Bowl.'

'What you do on holiday is your business,' Emily Glassover replied. 'I can't believe the EBU rules allow it. Whatever next?'

Play began and this was an early board:

```
Neither Vul.              ♠ 7 4 3
Dealer East               ♡ 10 7 5
                          ◇ 7 4 3
                          ♣ A K 7 3
        ♠ 8 2                            ♠ A J 10 9 6
        ♡ K J 9 6 4 2         N          ♡ Q
        ◇ —              W         E      ◇ Q 6 2
        ♣ Q 9 8 6 2          S          ♣ J 10 5 4
                          ♠ K Q 5
                          ♡ A 8 3
                          ◇ A K J 10 9 8 5
                          ♣ —
```

WEST	NORTH	EAST	SOUTH
Stan	*The*	*Emily*	*The*
Glassover	*Abbot*	*Glassover*	*Parrot*
—	—	2♠	5◇
All Pass			

Mrs Glassover opened 2♠, showing five spades and four or more cards in one of the minors. The Parrot's overcall of 5◇ was passed out and the ♠8 was led, East rising with the ace.

The Parrot paused to assess his prospects. If trumps broke 2-1, he would be able to cross to the ◇7 on the third round and discard both heart losers on the ♣A-K, scoring an overtrick. What if the trumps were 3-0? If West held three trumps and East switched to a heart at Trick 2 (which seemed likely), the game appeared to be doomed. What if East held all three trumps? Ah, it seemed that something could be done about that.

His calculations at an end, the Parrot unblocked the ♠Q under East's ♠A. He won the ♡Q switch with the ace and played the ace of trumps, West discarding a heart. The Parrot clicked his beak, happy with his play so far. East had surely started with 5-1-3-4 shape and could be end-played in spades. He cashed the ♠K to leave these cards still in play:

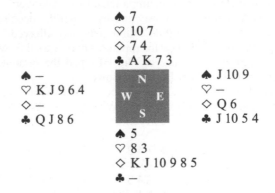

```
              ♠ 7
              ♡ 10 7
              ◇ 7 4
              ♣ A K 7 3
  ♠ —                        ♠ J 10 9
  ♡ K J 9 6 4      N         ♡ —
  ◇ —          W       E     ◇ Q 6
  ♣ Q J 8 6        S         ♣ J 10 5 4
              ♠ 5
              ♡ 8 3
              ◇ K J 10 9 8 5
              ♣ —
```

The Parrot exited with the ♠5, leaving Emily Glassover with no safe return. When she eventually led the ◇6, the Parrot won with dummy's ◇7 and discarded two hearts on the top clubs. He then drew the last trump and claimed the contract.

'You see?' said the Abbot. 'I told you he was a good player.'

'I still don't think it's right,' Emily Glassover replied. 'Just look at some of the younger players here. Tattoos and piercings, fake tans some of them. I prefer the good old days when all the men wore a jacket and tie. That's what Stan does.'

'Too hot for that!' screeched the Parrot, drawing a few glances from the adjacent tables.

'You should be used to it,' retorted Stan Glassover. 'You come from the jungle, don't you?'

The Abbot made no comment but he was far from happy with the man's attitude. Anyone would think he was a taxi driver!

A few boards later, the Parrot's card play was tested again:

East-West Vul.
Dealer South

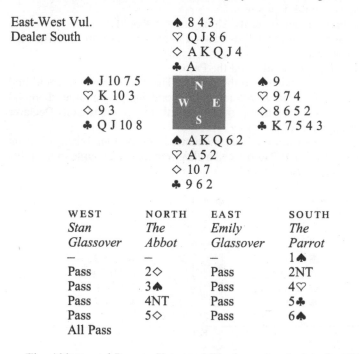

♠ 8 4 3
♡ Q J 8 6
◇ A K Q J 4
♣ A

♠ J 10 7 5
♡ K 10 3
◇ 9 3
♣ Q J 10 8

♠ 9
♡ 9 7 4
◇ 8 6 5 2
♣ K 7 5 4 3

♠ A K Q 6 2
♡ A 5 2
◇ 10 7
♣ 9 6 2

WEST	NORTH	EAST	SOUTH
Stan	*The*	*Emily*	*The*
Glassover	*Abbot*	*Glassover*	*Parrot*
–	–	–	1♠
Pass	2◇	Pass	2NT
Pass	3♠	Pass	4♡
Pass	4NT	Pass	5♣
Pass	5◇	Pass	6♠
All Pass			

The Abbot used Roman Key-card Blackwood to locate the ♡A and the ♠A-K-Q. Stan Glassover tossed the ♣Q on the table and down went the dummy.

The Parrot nodded his acceptance of the Abbot's bidding and paused to plan the play. If trumps were 3-2, he could score five spades, five diamonds, two aces and a club ruff for an overtrick. What if trumps were 4-1?

The Parrot won the first trick with the ♣A and called for a trump. The ♠9 appeared from East and the Parrot followed blithely with the ♠2. Stan Glassover raised an eyebrow. Had the strange bird meant to do that?

The Parrot won the heart switch with the ace and drew a second round of trumps, East showing out. He then ruffed a club in dummy and returned to his hand with the ◇10. After drawing the remaining trumps, he claimed the contract. 'Three losers go on diamonds,' he squawked.

Mrs Glassover was not entranced with the Parrot's overbearing manner. 'It's not very good etiquette to look so pleased with yourself,' she informed him. 'So what if you made twelve tricks? There was nothing we could do about it.'

The Parrot made no reply, shrugging his shoulders.

'If you're so clever, tell us how we could have beaten it,' demanded Stan Glassover.

'Diamond, diamond,' said the Parrot.

'That's true,' exclaimed the Abbot. 'There's no way you could find such a lead, I realize. If you lead a diamond and play another diamond when you take your trump trick, you kill the diamond suit. Declarer can't arrange his club ruff.'

The Abbot's team won this encounter 20-0 and found themselves on Table 2. Lucius and Paulo faced a clean-cut married couple in their 30s and this was an early board:

North-South Vul.
Dealer North

```
                    ♠ K J 7
                    ♡ 7 4 3
                    ◇ A Q 10 6 5
                    ♣ Q 6
     ♠ –                            ♠ A 5 2
     ♡ A Q J 5          N           ♡ 10 9 8 2
     ◇ K J 8 3 2    W       E       ◇ 9 7 4
     ♣ J 10 9 4         S           ♣ K 8 7
                    ♠ Q 10 9 8 6 4 3
                    ♡ K 6
                    ◇ –
                    ♣ A 5 3 2
```

WEST	NORTH	EAST	SOUTH
David	*Brother*	*Suzie*	*Brother*
Klemp	*Paulo*	*Klemp*	*Lucius*
–	1◇	Pass	1♠
Dble	Rdble	2♡	4♠
All Pass			

Brother Paulo showed three spades with his Support Redouble and David Klemp led the ♣J against the eventual spade game. Brother Lucius had no great wish for East to gain the lead. 'Small, please,' he said.

When the club jack was allowed to win, West was unwilling to switch to either red suit. He continued passively with the ♣4, drawing the queen, king and ace. Brother Lucius ruffed a club in dummy and discarded a heart on the ◇A. He then reached his hand with a diamond ruff and ruffed his last club with the ♠K. He continued with dummy's last trump and was soon able to claim the contract.

The smartly dressed Suzie Klemp returned her cards to the wallet. 'I see now why you played low from dummy at Trick 1,' she said. 'If it goes queen-king-ace instead, I can win the second round with the ♣8 and lead a heart through.'

Lucius nodded his agreement. 'With you holding the ace of trumps, I was lucky the suit was 3-0,' he replied. 'Otherwise your partner could cross to a trump for a heart switch.'

This turned out to be the key deal of the match:

East-West Vul.
Dealer South

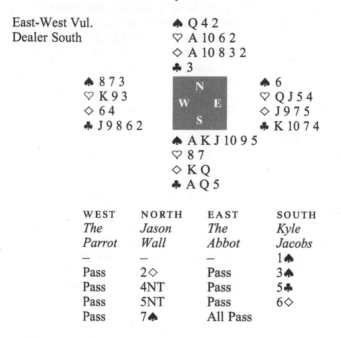

```
                    ♠ Q 4 2
                    ♡ A 10 6 2
                    ◇ A 10 8 3 2
                    ♣ 3
    ♠ 8 7 3                      ♠ 6
    ♡ K 9 3          N           ♡ Q J 5 4
    ◇ 6 4        W       E       ◇ J 9 7 5
    ♣ J 9 8 6 2      S           ♣ K 10 7 4
                    ♠ A K J 10 9 5
                    ♡ 8 7
                    ◇ K Q
                    ♣ A Q 5
```

WEST	NORTH	EAST	SOUTH
The	*Jason*	*The*	*Kyle*
Parrot	*Wall*	*Abbot*	*Jacobs*
–	–	–	1♠
Pass	2◇	Pass	3♠
Pass	4NT	Pass	5♣
Pass	5NT	Pass	6◇
Pass	7♠	All Pass	

The young North player used Roman Key-card Blackwood to locate three key-cards opposite and then the ◇K. After a few moments he decided to bid a grand slam in spades.

The Parrot studied his hand. North was presumably hoping that his diamond suit could be brought in. What should he lead? Leading a lame trump against a grand slam had been recommended by text-books through the ages. In his opinion such leads were overrated. Grand slams were likely to be cold 90% of the time. On the remaining 10% of deals an attack on dummy's entries stood a better chance of success.

Realizing that the Abbot would have something to say if the lead misfired, the Parrot stretched a claw towards his wooden cardholder and placed the ♡9 on the table.

The shaven-headed Kyle Jacobs was not happy to receive a heart lead. On a trump lead, he could ruff two clubs in dummy, draw trumps and unblock the diamond honours in his hand. He would then cross to the ♡A and discard his heart loser on the ◇A. 'Ace, please,' he said.

What options remained after this awkward lead? If trumps were 2-2, he could play the ♠A, unblock the diamonds and cross to the ♠Q. If diamonds didn't break 3-3, he could establish the thirteenth diamond with a ruff and re-enter dummy with a club ruff to discard his heart loser. The alternative was to play the ♠A, unblock the diamonds and continue with the ♠K and ♠Q. This would succeed when diamonds were 3-3. If the ◇J fell in two rounds, he would be OK on either line.

Declarer played the trump ace and his two top diamonds, the jack not appearing. Because the 4-2 divisions with a defender holding ◇J-x could be excluded, it was now better to play for diamonds 3-3 rather than trumps 2-2. Declarer played the king and queen of trumps and tested the diamonds. They failed to divide equally and he was one down.

Jason Wall, who had followed the play closely, turned towards the Parrot. 'What did you have in hearts?' he asked.

'King-nine-three,' replied the Parrot, who prided himself on his card memory.

'Wow, what a brilliant lead!' Wall exclaimed. 'I probably shouldn't say this but when we read about how well the Abbot was doing in the Bermuda Bowl, we couldn't believe it. Now I begin to understand.'

The Abbot's mouth fell open. Had these impertinent youngsters not seen the hand records from Chennai? Had all his brilliant plays against Meckstroth and Rodwell passed them by?

'Obvious lead,' retorted the Parrot. 'I never lead a trump against a grand slam!'

19.   The Star Attraction

After just two rounds, the Abbot's team was in the lead in the Winchester green-point Swiss.

'We've made an excellent start,' observed the Abbot. 'Still, one bad match and you can drop like a stone in this sort of event.'

From the Parrot's reaction, he didn't seem to think this very likely. 'Poor standard, poor standard,' he squawked, rocking from side to side.

The Abbot could not believe his luck when they faced two married couples in the third round. By what miracle had these unknown protagonists arrived at Table 1? He would do his utmost to ensure that their stay at such an exalted location was a short one.

This was an early board at the Abbot's table:

```
North-South Vul.              ♠ A 9 7
Dealer West                   ♡ 7 5 4
                              ◇ K 5 3 2
                              ♣ 8 4 3
        ♠ 5                 N                ♠ 6 4 3
        ♡ K Q J 9 3      W     E             ♡ 10 8 6 2
        ◇ J 10 8 6                           ◇ 9 7 4
        ♣ K J 7             S                ♣ 10 9 5
                              ♠ K Q J 10 8 2
                              ♡ A
                              ◇ A Q
                              ♣ A Q 6 2
```

WEST	NORTH	EAST	SOUTH
Myrtle	*The*	*Bob*	*The*
Greenway	*Abbot*	*Greenway*	*Parrot*
1♡	Pass	Pass	Dble
Pass	2◇	Pass	2♠
Pass	4♠	Pass	6♠
All Pass			

Myrtle Greenway stole a glance at the Parrot as he leapt to a slam. Goodness me, what wild bidding! Still, it was too much to hope that a trained bird would know how to use Blackwood. His overweight trainer had done well to teach him to play at all.

The Parrot won the ♡K lead with the ace, noting that West would surely hold all the outstanding honours. He crossed to the ♠7, ruffed a heart high and returned to dummy with the ♠9. After ruffing dummy's last heart, he drew a second round of trumps, West throwing a heart. These cards were still in play:

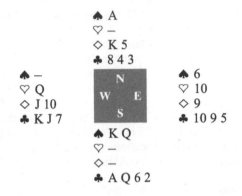

      ♠ A
      ♡ —
      ◇ K 5
      ♣ 8 4 3

♠ —   ♠ 6
♡ Q   ♡ 10
◇ J 10   ◇ 9
♣ K J 7   ♣ 10 9 5

      ♠ K Q
      ♡ —
      ◇ —
      ♣ A Q 6 2

East had signalled an even number of hearts at Trick 1, so it was impossible for West's ♣K to be doubleton. It seemed to the Parrot that the best chance was to find her with 1-5-4-3 shape. She would then have no safe discard on the next trick.

When the Parrot crossed to the ace of trumps, the ♡Q appeared from West. He continued with king and another diamond, discarding two clubs from his hand. Mrs Greenway won the fourth round of diamonds and had to lead a club into the Parrot's tenace. The slam had been made.

'Difficult for you, Myrtle,' said Rob Greenway. 'I think you do better to keep the ♡Q. Then you don't have to lead a club when he throws you in.'

'Throw club, I duck club!' squawked the Parrot, rocking disdainfully backwards and forwards. Saints alive . . . did they think he wouldn't be able to read the cards after a club discard?

'You're probably right, Bob,' said Mrs Greenway. 'I was put out of my stride when it jumped to a slam without bidding Blackwood. There was no reason to expect an ace in dummy after I'd opened the bidding.'

At the other table, Lucius and Paulo faced Mr and Mrs Elliott.

Neither Vul.
Dealer South

```
                    ♠ A 9
                    ♡ Q J 5 3 2
                    ◇ 8 7 4
                    ♣ 8 5 2
♠ Q J 10 6 5                        ♠ 8 7 3
♡ 10 7 4          N                 ♡ K 9 6
◇ K 5 3     W          E            ◇ J 10 9
♣ Q 4             S                 ♣ J 10 7 6
                    ♠ K 4 2
                    ♡ A 8
                    ◇ A Q 6 2
                    ♣ A K 9 3
```

WEST	NORTH	EAST	SOUTH
Brother	*Jennie*	*Brother*	*Clive*
Lucius	*Elliott*	*Paulo*	*Elliott*
–	–	–	2NT
Pass	3◇	Pass	3♡
Pass	3NT	All Pass	

Brother Lucius led the ♠Q and Clive Elliott, a local geography teacher, considered his prospects thoughtfully. It looked as if he would need four tricks from the heart suit. A 3-3 break would be welcome, obviously. Was there any other chance? Yes, if West held a doubleton king, that card would appear on the second round.

When the ♡A was led, Brother Paulo followed smoothly with the ♡9 in the East seat. Interesting card, thought Clive Elliott. He continued with the ♡8, which was covered by West's ♡10. Jennie Elliott leaned forward to play one of the dummy's heart honours.

'No, no, wait a minute,' her husband instructed. East's ♡9 was quite likely to be from ♡K-9 doubleton, wasn't it? If East had started with a singleton ♡9 or had played high from ♡9-7 or ♡9-6, it wouldn't be possible to score four heart tricks anyway. 'Play low, will you, Jennie.'

The geography teacher watched expectantly for the ♡K to appear from East but Brother Paulo kept him waiting, following with the ♡6. Somewhat surprised to win the trick with his 10, Brother Lucius cleared the spade suit. Not long afterwards, declarer had to concede two down.

'That's unlike you, Clive,' Jennie Elliott observed. 'Play one of my heart honours and you force out the king. Once you do that, you only need a 3-3 heart break to make the contract.'

At the other table, the Parrot had just reached game in a 5-2 fit:

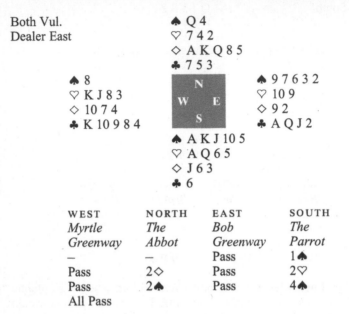

Both Vul.
Dealer East

♠ Q 4
♡ 7 4 2
◇ A K Q 8 5
♣ 7 5 3

♠ 8
♡ K J 8 3
◇ 10 7 4
♣ K 10 9 8 4

♠ 9 7 6 3 2
♡ 10 9
◇ 9 2
♣ A Q J 2

♠ A K J 10 5
♡ A Q 6 5
◇ J 6 3
♣ 6

WEST	NORTH	EAST	SOUTH
Myrtle	*The*	*Bob*	*The*
Greenway	*Abbot*	*Greenway*	*Parrot*
–	–	Pass	1♠
Pass	2◇	Pass	2♡
Pass	2♠	Pass	4♠
All Pass			

With the other three suits bid against her, Myrtle Greenway led the ♣10. On being assured that this card had won the trick, she continued with the ♣9. East overtook with the ♣J and the Parrot flicked the ♡5 onto the table.

Myrtle Greenway surveyed the Parrot with no great affection. Clever as it was for a household pet to play the game at all, was it too much to expect him to know that spades were trumps? If Bob was awake, he would surely play another club, hoping that the Parrot would give away another trick.

When the ♣A appeared next, the Parrot did indeed discard the ♡6. Seeing that a fourth round of clubs could be ruffed with dummy's ♠4, Bob Greenway switched to the ♡10. The Parrot won with the ♡A and drew trumps in five rounds, looking extremely pleased when the bad break came to light. Four rounds of diamonds allowed him to discard the ♡Q and the game was made.

The Parrot moved to his left, spying the ♡K in Mrs Greenway's remaining cards. 'Only way to make it!' he squawked.

The St Titus team preserved their lead with a 17-3 win and in the last match before the tea-break faced a team that had driven from London in search of green points.

'Ah, the famous Parrot!' exclaimed James Tythe, an accountant in London's Square Mile. 'I recognized you from the photo in that *Bridge Magazine* article. What are you doing here? Your Bermuda Bowl team comes from somewhere in Africa, doesn't it?'

The Abbot cleared his throat, hoping that the opponents would realize that he, too, had been part of the team.

'Just visiting,' replied the Parrot. 'AWFUL photo in *Bridge Magazine*! Made me look ancient.'

'Who cares about the photo?' said Roger Kitchen. 'It was all the great plays you made that amazed us. Do you remember that Five Hearts doubled contract against USA2, where you . . .'

'Shall we start?' said the Abbot stiffly. Good gracious, anyone would think that the Parrot had achieved their Bermuda Bowl success all on his own.

With deft moves of the beak the Parrot sorted his cards for the first board:

```
Both Vul.                  ♠ Q 4
Dealer East                ♡ 6 4
                           ◇ A Q J 10 9 5
                           ♣ A 5 4
        ♠ 10 8                            ♠ A K J 9 7
        ♡ Q 9 3          N                ♡ J 10
        ◇ 8 4         W     E             ◇ 7 6 2
        ♣ K 10 9 7 3 2      S             ♣ Q J 8
                           ♠ 6 5 3 2
                           ♡ A K 8 7 5 2
                           ◇ K 3
                           ♣ 6
```

WEST	NORTH	EAST	SOUTH
James	*The*	*Roger*	*The*
Tythe	*Abbot*	*Kitchen*	*Parrot*
–	–	1♠	2♡
Pass	3◇	Pass	3♡
Pass	4♡	All Pass	

James Tythe led the ♠10 and East overtook with the jack, switching to the jack of trumps. If trumps broke 3-2, the Parrot could see plenty of tricks in the red suits. He just needed to retain control of the spade suit. He won the trump switch and returned another spade, won by East's king. When another trump was returned, the Parrot won in his hand and turned to the diamond suit. Everyone followed to the first two rounds and he ditched one spade on the third round. West ruffed but had no spade to play. The Parrot won the club switch with dummy's ace and disposed of his last spade on a good diamond. The contract had been made.

'A trump lead is better, isn't it?' observed Roger Kitchen. 'He can't do it all, then.'

Tythe gathered his cards resignedly. 'Even a club is good enough,' he said.

Or a diamond lead, thought the Parrot, not that he would point this out after their kind words earlier.

Meanwhile, Lucius and Paulo faced competent opposition at the other table:

Both Vul.
Dealer East

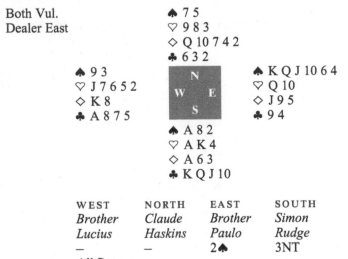

	♠ 7 5	
	♡ 9 8 3	
	◇ Q 10 7 4 2	
	♣ 6 3 2	
♠ 9 3		♠ K Q J 10 6 4
♡ J 7 6 5 2		♡ Q 10
◇ K 8		◇ J 9 5
♣ A 8 7 5		♣ 9 4
	♠ A 8 2	
	♡ A K 4	
	◇ A 6 3	
	♣ K Q J 10	

WEST	NORTH	EAST	SOUTH
Brother	Claude	Brother	Simon
Lucius	Haskins	Paulo	Rudge
–	–	2♠	3NT
All Pass			

Brother Lucius led the ♠9 and Claude Haskins displayed his dummy with an apologetic air. 'Not the best hand I've ever picked up,' he said. '*Bon chance!*'

Simon Rudge, who dressed extremely smartly for work in the City but switched to jeans and a tee-shirt for bridge, nodded his thanks. 'Play small,' he said.

Declarer ducked the first trick, allowing East's ♠10 to win, and won the spade continuation. To have any chance of making the contract, it seemed that West would have to hold the ♣A and seemingly a doubleton ◇K too. When he led the ♣K, Brother Lucius won immediately and switched to a low heart. Simon Rudge won East's

queen with the ace and then played the ◇A. After a few seconds'
thought Brother Lucius dropped his king under the ace.

The casually dressed declarer paused to assess the situation. West
would scarcely have dropped the king from a three-card holding, since
he could then have shut out the dummy by holding up the king on the
second round. It seemed likely that East had ◇J-9 or ◇J-8 remaining.
In that case perhaps he could catch him in an end-play.

Simon Rudge abandoned the diamond suit for the moment and
played his established winners in clubs. This was the position as the
last club was led:

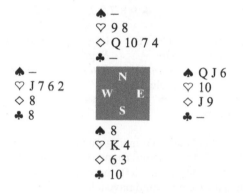

A heart was thrown from dummy and East discarded the ♡10.
Simon Rudge continued with the ♡K and Brother Paulo was forced to
discard a spade to retain his diamond guard. When he was thrown in
with a spade, he cashed one more winner in the suit and then had to lead
into dummy's diamond tenace. The game was made.

'You played it well,' exclaimed Brother Lucius. 'Better for us if I
lead a heart, I think.'

The last deal before the tea interval saw the Parrot in action once
more:

Neither Vul.
Dealer West

	♠ K 9 7 5	
	♡ J 8 7	
	◇ K J 8	
	♣ A K 5	

♠ 10	N	♠ J 8 6 3
♡ A K 9 6 3 2	W E	♡ Q 10 5
◇ A 7 4 3	S	◇ 9 5 2
♣ J 4		♣ Q 10 6

	♠ A Q 4 2	
	♡ 4	
	◇ Q 10 6	
	♣ 9 8 7 3 2	

WEST	NORTH	EAST	SOUTH
Jeremy	*The*	*Roger*	*The*
Tythe	*Abbot*	*Kitchen*	*Parrot*
1♡	Dble	2♡	2♠
3◇	3♠	Pass	4♠
All Pass			

After a not particularly convincing auction, the Parrot arrived in a spade game. He ruffed the second round of hearts and played the ace of trumps. When the ten fell on his left, there was every chance that it was a singleton. In that case he would have a loser in every suit. What could be done?

Abandoning trumps for the moment, the Parrot played a diamond to the king. When diamonds were continued, West took his ace and switched to the ♣4. 'Ace,' said the Parrot, who continued with a second heart ruff in his hand. The queen of trumps confirmed that trumps were 4-1 but there was a good chance of an end-play against East. The Parrot cashed his last diamond winner and exited with king and another club. East won with the queen and had to lead a trump into dummy's ♠K-9.

'Brilliant play!' exclaimed Roger Kitchen. 'You don't sign autographs, do you? If you could sign the back of my scorecard, that would mean a lot to me.'

The Abbot surveyed the scene in disbelief as the Parrot took hold of the proffered pen in his claw and scribbled some near-illegible signature. This event was not turning out as he had intended. They were doing very well, yes, but no-one had even mentioned the Bermuda Bowl to him. For some reason they were all too interested in his partner's antics. It was rather odd. No-one ever showed any interest in Brother Xavier.

20.   The Parrot's Grand Finale

The Abbot's team led the field by 13 VPs as they took their seats for the last round of the Winchester Green-point Swiss. 'I recognize these guys we're playing against,' the Abbot informed his team mates. 'Two of them are junior internationals. Heaven knows why they've come so far, just to play in a local event.'

'Ah, so now we face the famous Parrot,' exclaimed Luke Minton, offering his hand. 'Pleased to meet you! I'm afraid it took us rather a long time to reach Table 1.'

The Parrot leaned leftwards, proffering his right claw.

Simon Caulker smiled to himself. 'You know why we've come here, don't you?' he said. 'We're hoping to knock you off your perch. Not literally, of course!'

The Parrot was unamused. He sorted through his cards for the first board, finding that he had a 1NT opener:

N/S Vul.
Dealer South

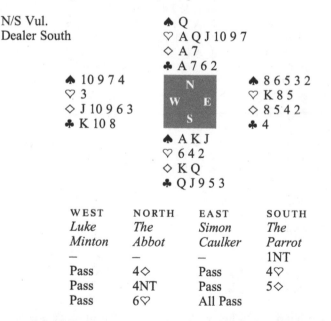

```
                    ♠ Q
                    ♡ A Q J 10 9 7
                    ◇ A 7
                    ♣ A 7 6 2
   ♠ 10 9 7 4                      ♠ 8 6 5 3 2
   ♡ 3                             ♡ K 8 5
   ◇ J 10 9 6 3                    ◇ 8 5 4 2
   ♣ K 10 8                        ♣ 4
                    ♠ A K J
                    ♡ 6 4 2
                    ◇ K Q
                    ♣ Q J 9 5 3
```

WEST	NORTH	EAST	SOUTH
Luke	*The*	*Simon*	*The*
Minton	*Abbot*	*Caulker*	*Parrot*
—	—	—	1NT
Pass	4◇	Pass	4♡
Pass	4NT	Pass	5◇
Pass	6♡	All Pass	

The Parrot arrived in 6♡ after a high-level transfer and the ◇J was led. He won in his hand and led trump to the queen, Simon Caulker following smoothly with the ♡8.

'Queen of spades,' said the Parrot, overtaking with the ace in his hand. He was about to lead another trump when a worrying thought came into his mind. What if the tiresome East, who fancied himself as a comedian, had held up from ♡K-8-5? When he took his trump trick, he would be able to lock declarer in the dummy! There would be no chance to take a club finesse.

The Parrot decided to guard against this situation. He cashed the ♠K, throwing the dummy's ◇A. Only then did he lead a second trump. When West discarded a diamond, the Parrot gave a satisfied click of the beak. Thank goodness he had played carefully! He won with the ♡A and threw East on lead with a third round of trumps. Simon Caulker then had to give the lead to declarer's hand, in spades or diamonds. The Parrot won the spade return with the jack, discarding a club from dummy. A second club was thrown on the ◇Q and a successful club finesse landed the slam.

The young opponents eyed the Parrot respectfully. Wow! He was every bit as good as the *Bridge Magazine* article had claimed.

Both Vul.
Dealer North

```
                    ♠ A K J 4
                    ♡ A 7 4
                    ◇ A J 4
                    ♣ A Q 2
  ♠ Q                                ♠ 10 8 6 3
  ♡ J 9 8 6 2          N             ♡ K 10 5 3
  ◇ 8 7 5 3         W     E          ◇ K 9 6
  ♣ 9 8 7              S             ♣ 5 3
                    ♠ 9 7 5 2
                    ♡ Q
                    ◇ Q 10 2
                    ♣ K J 10 6 4
```

WEST	NORTH	EAST	SOUTH
Luke	*The*	*Simon*	*The*
Minton	*Abbot*	*Caulker*	*Parrot*
–	2♣	Pass	2◇
Pass	2NT	Pass	3♣
Pass	3♠	Pass	5♠
Pass	6♠	All Pass	

Turning a blind eye to his weak trumps, the Parrot made a general slam try of 5♠. The Abbot surveyed his cards learnedly. If five out of five key cards wasn't enough to bid the slam, he didn't know what was! Simon Caulker led a low trump and the Parrot laid out his dummy.

The Abbot nodded his approval of the cards on display. He won West's
♠Q with the ♠A and saw that there would be no need to take a
diamond finesse. He could discard two diamonds on dummy's clubs. If
he could manage two heart ruffs as well, there would be an easy
overtrick.

The Abbot cashed the ♡A and ruffed a heart. A club to the ace
allowed him to ruff his remaining heart and he then led dummy's last
trump, West showing out. So much for the overtrick, thought the Abbot
as he won with the trump king. In fact, wait a minute, was the contract
in trouble now?

The Abbot drew one more round of trumps with the jack. In the
unlikely case that East held four clubs, he would be able to ditch both
his diamond losers before East could ruff in. It was surely a better idea
to cross to dummy on the second round of clubs and take the 50%
chance of the diamond finesse.

The Abbot crossed to the ♣J and ran the ◇Q. When the finesse lost,
East drew the Abbot's last trump and returned a heart, West cashing
two tricks to put the slam three down.

The Parrot was hopping up and down in disbelief. 'Duck, duck,
duck!' he screeched.

The Abbot winced as the players at the adjacent tables turned their
heads. What on earth was the Parrot talking about? Duck what?

'He's right,' said Luke Minton. 'If you let my queen of trumps hold,
you can win the return, ruff two hearts, draw trumps and score all the
clubs.'

The Abbot returned his cards to the board. It seemed the other
players' analysis was right. He could afford to lose a trump trick and
should have done this at a moment when the defenders could do no
damage. Thanks goodness they had a lead of 13 VPs! Surely they could
survive one poor board.

At the other table, Lucius and Paulo faced two junior international
players:

Neither Vul.
Dealer East

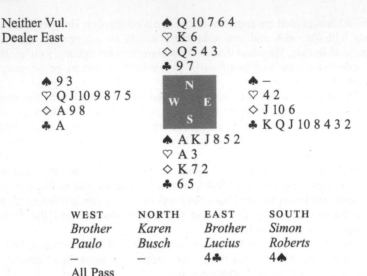

	♠ Q 10 7 6 4	
	♡ K 6	
	◇ Q 5 4 3	
	♣ 9 7	

♠ 9 3		♠ —
♡ Q J 10 9 8 7 5		♡ 4 2
◇ A 9 8		◇ J 10 6
♣ A		♣ K Q J 10 8 4 3 2

	♠ A K J 8 5 2	
	♡ A 3	
	◇ K 7 2	
	♣ 6 5	

WEST	NORTH	EAST	SOUTH
Brother	*Karen*	*Brother*	*Simon*
Paulo	*Busch*	*Lucius*	*Roberts*
–	–	4♣	4♠

All Pass

Brother Paulo led the ♣A and Brother Lucius followed with a middling ♣8. Declarer won the ♡Q switch in his hand and played the ♠A. Brother Paulo had no great wish to be end-played with the ♠9 and quickly disposed of this card. When East threw a club on this trick, the declarer looked respectfully at his left-hand opponent. Hmm . . . unblocking the nine. Monks or not, these guys played a strong game.

Declarer drew the last trump and led a diamond to the queen. He continued with dummy's ♡K, leaving these cards to be played:

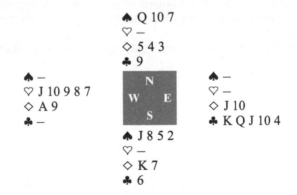

	♠ Q 10 7	
	♡ —	
	◇ 5 4 3	
	♣ 9	

♠ —		♠ —
♡ J 10 9 8 7		♡ —
◇ A 9		◇ J 10
♣ —		♣ K Q J 10 4

	♠ J 8 5 2	
	♡ —	
	◇ K 7	
	♣ 6	

Simon Roberts paused to consider his next play. If East had failed to unblock the honour from ◇J-6, an exit in either minor would succeed.

If East had begun with a singleton diamond, a club exit would be required. The final chance was that West had ◇A-J doubleton remaining; in that case a diamond exit would yield the contract.

Simon Roberts decided to call for a diamond. When the ◇J appeared from East, he played low from his hand. Brother Lucius cashed a club and led a third round of diamonds for one down.

'Could I have made it?' asked the declarer.

Brother Lucius shook his head. 'I don't think so,' he replied. Not once my partner ditches the ♠9.'

Simon Roberts nodded his appreciation of the position. If West had not unblocked in trumps, an eventual throw-in to his ♠9 would have been successful. A diamond exit would allow declarer to score three diamond tricks, discarding his club loser. If instead West chose to exit with a heart, declarer would ruff in the dummy and discard a diamond from his hand. He could then establish dummy's thirteenth diamond for a club discard.

The last board of the event arrived and the Abbot saw that he held a 20-count. Excellent! Surely he would become declarer and could display his expertise just before lifting the silver trophy.

The Abbot opened 2NT and the next player passed. The Parrot stretched out a claw and with some difficulty lifted a number of bidding cards from his box. The Abbot leaned forward to see what he had bid. Goodness me, what a selfish response! He had grabbed the contract in 5♣. This was the deal:

Both Vul.
Dealer North

```
                    ♠ 8 7 5 2
                    ♡ A Q 4 3
                    ◇ A K 7
                    ♣ A K
    ♠ Q J 10 4          N          ♠ K 6 3
    ♡ J 9 6 5                      ♡ K 10 8 2
    ◇ J 9 8 3      W       E       ◇ Q 10 4
    ♣ 5                            ♣ Q 7 2
                        S
                    ♠ A 9
                    ♡ 7
                    ◇ 6 5 2
                    ♣ J 10 9 8 6 4 3
```

WEST	NORTH	EAST	SOUTH
Luke	*The*	*Simon*	*The*
Minton	*Abbot*	*Caulker*	*Parrot*
–	2NT	Pass	5♣
All Pass			

The Parrot won the ♠Q lead with the ace and saw that all would be well if the trump queen fell in two rounds. Indeed, an overtrick might then be possible if the heart finesse succeeded. Mind you, the East player was looking pleased with himself, almost as pleased as after his fatuous 'knock you off your perch' joke. It certainly seemed that he had some hopes of beating the contract.

The Parrot crossed to the ♡A and ruffed a heart in his hand. His next move was to surrender a spade trick, won by West's ♠10. When West switched to a trump, the Parrot won in dummy and ruffed another heart in his hand. A diamond to the ace allowed him to ruff dummy's last heart with a high trump, all following.

Continuing to play at top speed, the Parrot returned to dummy with the ◇K and ruffed a spade in his hand. These cards were still in play:

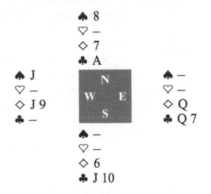

```
              ♠ 8
              ♡ —
              ◇ 7
              ♣ A
  ♠ J                        ♠ —
  ♡ —        N               ♡ —
  ◇ J 9    W     E           ◇ Q
  ♣ —        S               ♣ Q 7
              ♠ —
              ♡ —
              ◇ 6
              ♣ J 10
```

West showed out when a trump was played to the ace but this caused the Parrot no anxiety at all. Indeed, it meant that his exotic line of play had been the only one to land the contract. 'Spade!' he squawked.

Whichever minor-suit queen East chose to play, declarer's ♣J would be promoted for the eleventh trick. The club game had been made.

Turning towards the East player, the Parrot stretched out his wings in a magnificent display of blue and yellow. 'Notice anything?' he enquired.

'Sorry?' mumbled Simon Caulker. 'What do you mean?'

The Parrot restored his wings to their position of rest. 'I'm still on my perch!' he said.